WARFARE IN NEW KINGDOM EGYPT

WARFARE IN NEW KINGDOM EGYPT

PAUL ELLIOTT

FONTHILL

Fontonthill Media Language Policy

Fonthill Media publishes in the international English language market. One language edition is published worldwide. As there are minor differences in spelling and presentation, especially with regard to American English and British English, a policy is necessary to define which form of English to use. The Fonthill Policy is to use the form of English native to the author. Paul Elliott was born and educated in the UK; therefore British English has been adopted in this publication.

Fonthill Media Limited
Fonthill Media LLC
www.fonthillmedia.com
office@fonthillmedia.com

First published in the United Kingdom and the United States of America 2017

British Library Cataloguing in Publication Data:
A catalogue record for this book is available from the British Library

ISBN 978-1-78155-580-4

Typeset in 10pt on 13pt Sabon
Printed and bound in England

CONTENTS

Chronology

The list that follows indicates the divisions of Egyptian history and names all of the pharaohs of the New Kingdom, providing approximate dates for their reigns. Where dates overlap, the dynasties co-existed, carving up Egypt into multiple competing kingdoms. Most dates are computed from king lists, in particular those from the Turin royal papyrus with additional evidence from other sources (including key astronomical events). This chronology is taken from John Baines and Jaromir Malek's *Atlas of Ancient Egypt* and synthesises dates from the accepted middle and lower dating schemes.

Old Kingdom: 2,575–2,134 BC
First Intermediate Period: 2,134–2,040 BC
Middle Kingdom: 2,040–1,640 BC
- Eleventh Dynasty (all of Egypt)
  - Montuhotep II: 2,061–2,010 BC
  - Montuhotep III: 2,010–1,998 BC
  - Montuhotep IV: 1,998–1,991 BC
- Twelfth Dynasty
  - Amenhemet I: 1,991–1,962 BC
  - Sensuret I: 1,971–1,926 BC
  - Amenhemet II: 1,929–1,892 BC
  - Sensuret II: 1,897–1,878 BC
  - Sensuret III: 1,878–1,841 BC
  - Amenhemet III: 1,844–1,797 BC
  - Amenhemet IV: 1,799–1,787 BC
  - Queen Sobeknefru: 1,787–1,783 BC
- Thirteenth Dynasty (around seventy kings ruling from 1,783 to 1,640 BC)
- Fourteenth Dynasty (a dynasty of minor kings, ruling from the eastern Delta contemporaneous with the Thirteenth and Fifteenth Dynasties)

Second Intermediate Period: 1,640–1,532 BC
- Fifteenth Dynasty
  - Sheshi; Yakhuber; Khyan
  - Apophis: *c.* 1,585–1,542 BC
  - Khamudi: *c.* 1,542–1,532 BC

Sixteenth Dynasty
Minor Hyksos kings, ruling simultaneously with Fifteenth Dynasty
Anather; Yakobaam
Seventeenth Dynasty: Numerous kings ruling Upper Egypt from Thebes between 1,640–1,550 BC; the most notable being:
Sobekemsaf II; Nubkheperre Intef
Seqenenre Tao: *c.* 1,556 BC
Kamose: 1,555–1,550 BC
New Kingdom: 1,550–1,070 BC
Eighteenth Dynasty
Ahmose: 1,550–1,525 BC
Amenhotep I: 1,525–1,504 BC
Tuthmosis I: 1,504–1,492 BC
Tuthmosis II: 1,492–1,479 BC
Tuthmosis III: 1,479–1,425 BC
Queen Hatshepsut: 1,473–1,458 BC
Amenhotep II: 1,427–1,401 BC
Tuthmosis IV: 1,401–1,391 BC
Amenhotep III: 1,391–1,353 BC
Amenhotep IV/Akhenaten: 1,353–1,335 BC
Smenkhkare: 1,335–1,333 BC
Tutankhamun: 1,333–1,323 BC
Ay: 1,323–1,319 BC
Horemheb: 1,319–1,307 BC
Nineteenth Dynasty
Ramses I: 1,307–1,306 BC
Seti I: 1,306–1,290 BC
Ramses II: 1,290–1,224 BC
Merenptah: 1,224–1,214 BC
Seti II: 1,214–1,204 BC
Amenmesses, usurper during the reign of Seti I
Siptah: 1,204–1,198 BC
Queen Twosret: 1,198–1,196 BC
Twentieth Dynasty
Setnakhte: 1,196–1,194 BC
Ramses III: 1,194–1,163 BC
Ramses IV: 1,163–1,156 BC
Ramses V: 1,156–1,151 BC
Ramses VI: 1,151–1,143 BC
Ramses VII: 1,143–1,136 BC
Ramses VIII: 1,136–1,131 BC
Ramses IX: 1,131–1,112 BC
Ramses X: 1,112–1,100 BC
Ramses XI: 1,100–1,070 BC
Third Intermediate Period: 1,070–712 BC
Late Period: 712–332 BC
Greco-Roman Period: 332 BC–AD 395

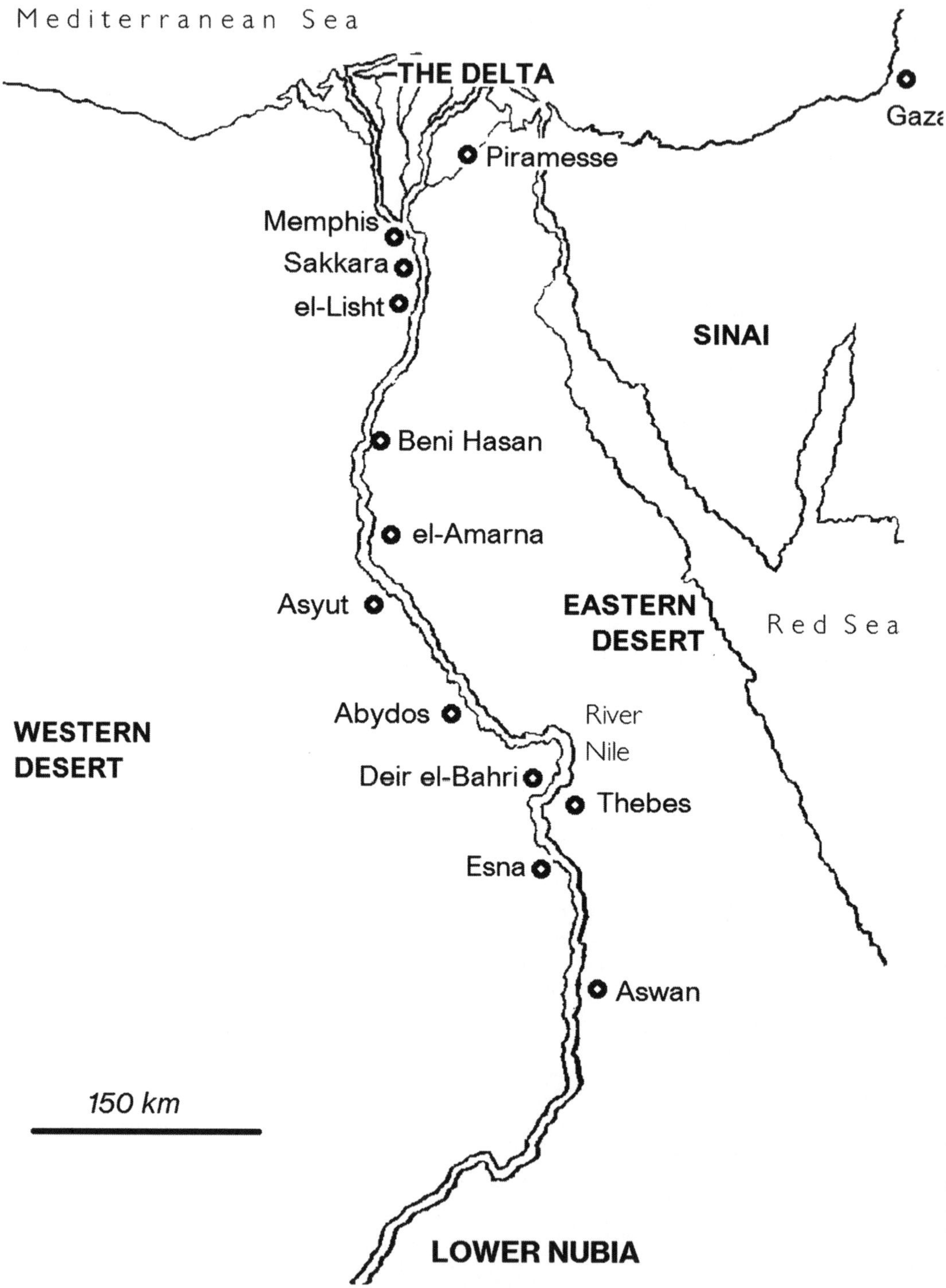
Mediterranean Sea
THE DELTA
Gaza
Piramesse
Memphis
Sakkara
el-Lisht
SINAI
Beni Hasan
el-Amarna
Asyut
EASTERN DESERT
Red Sea
Abydos
River Nile
WESTERN DESERT
Deir el-Bahri
Thebes
Esna
Aswan
150 km
LOWER NUBIA

Introduction

Studies of the Egyptian military have, in the past, tended to concentrate on the very few big battles that we know of, with very little interest shown in the technology of war and the way in which it was waged. This is perhaps partly due to the vast wealth of Egyptian subject matter available for study: tax records, religious practices, architecture, textiles, mummification, and dynastic history—both the epigraphic and the archaeological evidence is abundant. Studies of the Roman army, meanwhile, have come on apace in the last 100 years. Sword and helmet typologies have been constructed, individual blades measured and compared, and treatises written on the evolution of sword shapes and shield designs. In Britain, H. Russell Robinson pioneered the study of Roman helmets, fitting every extant example into a useful set of divisions and subdivisions, making future identifications easier. Dr Mike Bishop has made fantastic strides in untangling the complexities of legionary *lorica segmentata* armour, and, along with John Coulston, has written what could be called the 'Bible' of Roman military study: *Roman Military Equipment*, published by Oxbow Books.

Egyptology has always lacked that forensic analysis of its military artefacts, and there are no easily accessible typological assessments of sword types or evolutionary diagrams charting the development of composite bows or axe heads. Published drawings of many of the military artefacts in Egypt's museums do not exist, and likewise there are few decent photographs of the collections available. These are the problems, but despite a good source of accurate drawings and clear photographs, enough material has been studied in detail to enable us to make a tentative start on a study of Egyptian weaponry and warfare.

Warfare in New Kingdom Egypt does not pretend to be all-encompassing and to analyse the Egyptian way of war across its tremendously long history. I have focused on the New Kingdom for very clear reasons. Warfare in the Old and Middle Kingdoms (that period of pyramid building when Egypt had little contact with foreign powers) changed little over time, and although fascinating in itself, it lacked the complexity and influences that gripped the military men of the New Kingdom. This later period of Egyptian history encompassed the aggressive reigns of warrior pharaohs like Seti I, Amenhotep III, Tuthmosis III and IV, and, of course, Ramses II ('the Great'). The New Kingdom shifted its interests south to Thebes and poured resources into that famous tomb complex within the Valley of the Kings. Military planners of the Old Kingdom had been conservative, parochial, and short-sighted, while those of the New Kingdom were aggressive, innovative, and outward-looking. Exactly why this is the subject of the first two chapters of the book, for only understanding the military system that had lain in place before the New Kingdom can one really understand how radical was the system that replaced it.

Without doubt, the expansionist pharaohs of the New Kingdom ruled over an Egyptian superpower and they butted heads with equally powerful kings ruling their own military states. Much of the diplomacy and warfare between these super-states took place across the Near East (running in an arc known as the 'Fertile Crescent', from Gaza and Israel, through Lebanon, Syria, and into Northern Iraq). Relatively few battles of any note took place on Egyptian soil, the exception being the invasions of Libyans and an enigmatic group known as the Sea Peoples, close to the end of the New Kingdom. Who these people were and what they wanted has always proven a historical conundrum of the first order. However, the results of their repulsion from Egypt by the forces of pharaoh had long-lasting effects. Ramses III and his highly organised army defeated the invaders but did not destroy them, with the consequence that they then seized lands and cities across the Fertile Crescent. Ancient kingdoms fell, cities were burned to the ground, and the old established order swept away. Egypt no longer had the territories it had taken by force centuries earlier, and without these treaty states, allied cities, conquered areas, and imperial possessions, Egypt shrank. Raw materials were difficult to source, taxes were curtailed, and the flow of high-quality bows, chariots, suits of armour, and war horses sent as tribute to the Egyptian armouries dried up too. Egypt had become poorer and less able to sustain its well-equipped military garrisons, with the result that it became inward-looking once again.

What followed the New Kingdom is known by Egyptologists today as the Late Period, and it is generally understood to be a time of decline coupled with periods of foreign invasion. Burgeoning civilisations like Meroe, Assyria, Persia, Greece, and Rome were all able to take advantage of Egypt's fall from power.

On my visits to Egypt across a span of twenty years, I have met some wonderful people and expert guides, but I would like to thank in particular Mohamed Monem Basha (Luxor) and Abdul Moez Sebak Mahmoud (Cairo), who assisted me on my most recent trip. Thanks also to the friendly staff of the Oriental Museum at Durham University, to Ilona Regulski and others at the British Museum in London, and to Professor Joann Fletcher of the University of York.

Paul Elliott

1

Warfare in the Middle Kingdom

Come, let me describe to you the ills of the soldier...

Lesson in letter writing by Nebmare-nakht

Howard Carter's discovery of the tomb of Pharaoh Tutankhamun in 1922 was rightly hailed as the greatest archaeological find of the century; almost 100 years later, the find must stand as the greatest archaeological discovery ever made. The 'wonderful things' brought to light by Carter's hard work dazzled and electrified the world and sparked a Western demand for everything Egyptian. Clothes, jewellery, hairstyles, fabrics, furniture, and architecture were all influenced by Egyptian motifs throughout the 1920s—President Herbert Hoover even named his pet dog after the Egyptian boy king.

The American Egyptologist Herbert Winlock had been a friend of Carter's and played some part in the political negotiations that took place once Tutankhamun's tomb had been opened. Winlock worked for the Metropolitan Museum of Art, and he was particularly interested in the Middle Kingdom of Egypt, which led him to the cliffs of Deir el-Bahri, on the West Bank of the Nile, opposite Luxor. In 1923, only a year on from Carter's breath-taking discoveries in the Valley of the Kings, Winlock's team located a previously unknown rock-cut tomb at Deir el-Bahri and tentatively made their way in. Inside there were no elaborate grave goods, no gold, no chariots, or alabaster jars; there were, however, mummies—a mass of intermingled and partially mummified bodies that were so decayed that they reeked when they were laid out in the hot sun. Winlock thought that the putrefying bodies might actually be the remains of Coptic monks and declared his findings to be too 'gruesome'. Crestfallen, the Egyptologist had the tomb sealed. It was not until three years later, in 1926, that the mummies were more carefully examined. On closer inspection, it appeared that there were actually sixty separate corpses within the tomb and that they all dated from the end of the Middle Kingdom. Once a professor of anatomy, Dr Douglas Derry of the

Kasr el-Ainy Medical School in Cairo, became involved and spent time at the dig site studying the bodies, it became clear that the men were actually soldiers. All of the bodies showed signs of a violent death, including fractures and puncture wounds from arrows. Shockingly, some of the arrowheads still remained within the mummies and were picked out by the amazed doctor. Although Derry thought the men to be native Egyptians, Winlock instead identified them by their hairstyles as Nubians, from the land on Egypt's southern border that served as a common source of mercenaries for the army.

What were the partially mummified remains of sixty Nubian warriors doing in an unfinished rock-cut tomb meant for a Middle Kingdom nobleman? The perfectly preserved bodies of numerous Egyptian queens, kings, and princelings had been studied over the decades, but here was a chance to examine corpses from some unnamed ancient battle, a rare glimpse into the harsh realities of brutal Bronze Age warfare. Could the bodies of these slain soldiers tell us anything about Egyptian weapons and warfare?

Based on dental examination, the men all seem to have been aged between thirty and forty and three of them had greying hair. All of the corpses had suffered severe injuries that led to their deaths, but Douglas Derry also noted the presence of older scars—evidence of past combat wounds that had healed. These men were veteran soldiers who had not survived their last battle. At the time, Winlock determined that the soldiers had probably died in the service of Pharaoh Montuhotep II (2,061–2,010 BC), whose temple was found nearby. Montuhotep had reunified Egypt following a period of civil war during the Middle Kingdom period of Egyptian history. His final victory, leading the troops of Thebes in victory against the rival city of Herakleopolis, had brought about a successful reunification. Perhaps, theorised Winlock, the troops were killed during the attack on the city, and as a reward for their loyalty, Montuhotep had the sixty bodies collected from the battlefield and interred within an unfinished tomb close to his own mortuary temple at Thebes. More recent studies cast doubt on such a precise identification for the battle in which the warriors participated. It is more likely that the soldiers died in some military confrontation much closer to Thebes and they were quickly and shoddily buried in a single mass grave. Some of the corpses had flesh removed and eyes pecked out by carrion birds, suggesting that they had lain on the battlefield for some time before being collected; in addition, the large amount of sand found on the bodies suggests only scant cleaning and preparation took place before the remains were wrapped in linen. In some cases, rigor mortis had made the hasty attempts at wrapping difficult—note that rigor mortis takes hold within an hour or two of death and lasts for up to two days (less in a hot climate).

It is fitting to begin an exploration of ancient Egyptian warfare by looking at its traumatic physical effects on the bodies of its victims. It is easy to become fascinated by the artistry of bronze scimitar swords, the elegance and beauty of Tutankhamun's war chariots, and the glorious hyperbole of Egyptian kings

An archer takes careful aim. He wears a bracer or wristguard that is designed to protect the wrist from the occasional 'slap' of the bowstring against the arm.

carved onto their own monuments. Yet war, reduced down to its basics, is about killing people or the threat to kill—the sixty slain soldiers of Montuhotep II remind us of this brutal fact.

It was evident that these fallen warriors were archers, mainly from the leather bracers that were found with the bodies, but also from two bowstrings and the tip of a bow that was also found among the debris. It is therefore ironic that they met their fate in a hailstorm of arrows shot at them by an enemy force. One soldier had been struck on the left side of his skull by an arrow and the force of the impact cracked open the bone, which still adhered to the inside of his cranial cavity. Another man had been struck by an arrow on the left side of his body, it had cut through flesh straight between the ribs and penetrated deeply into both his left lung and his heart; the arrow tip had protruded from the man's chest, but the impact of his body hitting the ground had actually snapped off the end of the blade.

Like a low-velocity bullet, an arrow does not simply hit bare flesh and stop, it penetrates deeply, often continuing its flesh-rending journey until it hits bone. In one case, an arrow had come down almost vertically, cutting through the victim's neck until the arrowhead had come to rest against his sternum.

In a shot that was reminiscent of the battle injuries described by Homer in *The Iliad*, one warrior had been struck full in the face, where it passed beneath his left eye socket, penetrated past the back of his nose, and into the back of his head. Death after such an awful injury would not have necessarily been fatal.

Stringing the bow.

The Roman writer Procopius described the fate of a legionary officer who was wounded during the siege of Rome in AD 537:

> The point of the arrow penetrated (his face) as far as the neck behind, but it did not show through, but the rest of the shaft projected from his face.... The physicians wished to draw the weapon from his face but were reluctant to do so, not so much on account of the eye, which they supposed could not be saved, but for fear lest, by cutting the membranes and tissues such as are very numerous in that region, they should cause the death of a man....
>
> Procopius of Caesarea
> History of the Wars

Amazingly, the physician Theoctistus was able to remove the arrow and save the soldier's eye; he even returned to duties without a scar.

Several of the mummies had been struck in the lungs and the ribs, and the large amount of bleeding associated with these particular bodies suggests that they did not die quickly but lay wounded for some time on the battlefield. This tallies with other evidence that, in the end, many of the wounded Nubians had actually been clubbed or stabbed to death. Some of these brutal injuries were post-mortem, suggesting that the victorious enemy overran the defeated Nubian troops, massacring the wounded and at the same time making sure that everyone else was truly dead.

The cuts and blows were aimed mainly at the head and were certainly savage and forceful, resulting in both skull fractures and broken noses. Spears and maces were perhaps the most likely weapons used by the attackers. Isolated fractures in a number of the victim's forearms indicate that some had strength enough at the very end to defend themselves as the blows rained down upon them. Most of the soldiers had suffered these secondary wounds to the side of the head, almost as if they had been held by the hair off the ground and struck on the side of the head by some blunt weapon, like a mace, that was swung with force by a right-handed attacker. Pharaohs often portray themselves smiting enemies in this way, and in the *Story of Sinuhe*, concerning the eponymous Egyptian traveller and adventurer, a graphic account is provided of such a *coup de grâce*. Sinuhe finds himself in a deadly duel with the champion of the Retennu people; he related: 'When he charged at me, I shot him, my arrow fixed into his neck. He screamed and fell on his nose; I despatched him with his own battle-axe' (Papyrus Berlin 10499, 3022 B 138–140). Sinuhe's account is a chilling parallel of the way in which some of the Nubian mummies were despatched.

Once the victors had moved on, the Nubians lay stretched out on the battlefield long enough for vultures to peck at the bodies. Within a day or so, however, allies arrived and carried the bodies to Deir el-Bahri. Winlock suggested a trip of more than 200 kilometres from Herakleopolis, but it is far more likely that the battlefield lay only a few kilometres away from the burial site. None of the bodies were mummified or embalmed by Egyptian priests of the dead; instead, they had been dried by the desert sun, covered in sand, and then wrapped in linen. It is doubtful that much time was wasted in getting the bodies into the tomb, although we should note that fragments of two wooden coffins were found by Winlock's team, suggesting that two of the Nubians, perhaps unit commanders, merited a more fitting burial within the tomb.

We can actually see what this platoon of Nubian archers may have looked like; two wooden models showing groups of soldiers were found within the tomb of Mesehti at Asyut in 1894. The first depicts a unit of Egyptian spearmen, while the second depicts a group of forty Nubian archers. All of the men carry a self bow in their left hand and a clutch of arrows in their right. Mesehti was probably a local prince or general based at Asyut around 2,000 BC, and the models buried with him may have represented part of his own personal army. Montuhotep II and Mesehti lived in the same tumultuous period of Egyptian history, known by the dry and sanitised name of the First Intermediate Period (2,134–2,040 BC)—it involved nothing less than a chaotic break-up of the Egyptian kingdom.

The First Intermediate Period represents the first great catastrophe in Egyptian history. It was a time of civil war, starvation, and poverty, brought on by a series of weak kings and a failing administration that was faced with two powerful threats. The first was most likely a series of disastrous harvests, coupled with widespread famine, while the second was a shift of power to the provincial governors (the nomarchs) who had over centuries treated their estates as personal fiefdoms to be defended by force and to be handed down to their sons. The glories of the pyramid age were replaced by competing warlords, many of whom declared themselves 'pharaoh', but who could never extend their rule far enough to encompass the whole of Egypt. All of these warring dynasties were weak and fought one another, with their own standing armies supplemented by mercenaries brought into Egypt from foreign lands. Both the wooden Nubians found inside Mesehti's tomb and the real life Nubians found partially mummified at Deir el-Bahri represent these freelance fighting forces. The fragmentary evidence we have of this chaotic period paints an apocalyptic picture; desperate crowds of refugees wandered from town to town in search of food, and petty kings and princelings defended the resources around them with force. There is at least one instance of cannibalism. In this age of poverty, violence, and desperation, 'when the Nile was empty and men crossed over it on foot', Egypt had reached its lowest ebb.

The rulers of Thebes, an important province (or nome) in the south, had for a century been able to extend their power northwards first to Abydos and then to Antaeopolis. Finally, the border of Theban territory reached almost as far as Asyut, the home of the prince Mesehti. Asyut sits on the Nile midway between Cairo and Aswan and marks the point at which power over the northern part of the Nile valley was held by Herakleopolis. In 2,061 BC, a new king of Thebes marched out with his troops to make war on Herakleopolis; he was Nebhetepre, but he adopted the regnal name of Montuhotep—meaning 'Montu is content'. Montu was the Theban god of war and Montuhotep would satisfy his god with an aggressive military campaign directed at the rival territories of the north. By the thirty-ninth year of his long reign, the Theban king had successfully defeated Herakleopolis, making him the undisputed king of Egypt. At last, Montuhotep could call himself 'Uniter of the Two Lands'. His mortuary temple sits in the great bay of rock at Deir el-Bahri, next to the much later and more frequently visited temple of Queen Hatshepsut.

Armies of the Middle Kingdom

Montuhotep is considered the first pharaoh of the Middle Kingdom, a strong and resurgent period of Egyptian history and one in which military campaigns were sent abroad and defences erected along the Egyptian frontiers. During the peace of the Old Kingdom, Egypt had been insulated from the outside world by the natural barriers that surrounded it on all sides: deserts to the east and west, the Mediterranean Sea to the north, and a series of river rapids that prevented ships sailing north out of Nubia. Unfortunately, the First Intermediate Period had seen neighbouring peoples take advantage of the chaos and disorder to cross over the border and infiltrate Egypt. Following the reunification of the kingdom, the Middle Kingdom pharaohs had to plug these gaps and were forced to pay attention to the defence of Egypt, investing in border forts, small standing armies, and a well-organised system of provincial militias, which could be summoned to war when needed.

The provincial nomes would form the core of pharaoh's army. Each nome equated to a single agricultural basin, requiring a large degree of central organisation to manage the complex tasks of irrigation. Nomes were effective political units and they formed the basis of Egypt's local government. Twenty were spread out across Lower Egypt, which contained the complex waterways of the Nile Delta, and there were a further twenty-two nomes strung out along the Nile valley, from Memphis at the apex of the Delta southwards to the First Cataract, the official southern border of ancient Egypt. Each governor of a nome is today referred to as a nomarch.

Men would be conscripted for a year or two and then return to their trades or to the fields from which they came. They were not professional soldiers, but joined a militia (*niwt*) that was raised by the nomarch. Pharaohs like Sensuret III (who campaigned aggressively in Nubia) or Amenemhet II (who led expeditions to the Red Sea) relied on their nomarchs to raise a force of suitably trained and disciplined levy troops. Thuthotep, for example, a nomarch of Pharaoh Sensuret, recorded that he had mustered the 'youthful recruits from the west of the Hare nome', as well as those 'from the east of the Hare nome' and the 'youths of the warriors from the Hare nome'. We should imagine that any nome that sat astride the Nile would have an automatic division of troops into two bodies, east and west. Troop contingents would vary in size with the population of the nome that they were raised from. The Hare nome was the fifteenth nome of Upper Egypt and not a densely settled part of the Nile valley; militias raised at Thebes, Memphis, or sites in the Delta would have been much larger. The 'youths of the warriors' that are mentioned by Thuthotep were the sons of hereditary fighters and represent the next generation of full-time professional soldiers (*ahautyu*). Depictions of *ahautyu* in tomb paintings from Beni Hasan, Mier, and El Berseh show them wearing a distinctive red ostrich plume fitted to a head-band. Militia forces would supplement and support these professional soldiers during large battles.

Nomarchs would be expected to lead the forces they had raised from their own territories, and one Amenemhet, a governor of the Oryx nome, is recorded as having led 6,000 'of all the bravest of the Oryx nome' on a campaign that was actually commanded by the pharaoh's vizier. They could also be commissioned by the pharaoh to act on his behalf, using the militia forces to protect the nome's frontiers from hostile tribes, undertake trade missions to distant lands, or obtain stone from remote desert quarries. In peacetime, the large repository of labour that was made up of all those young recruits (*hewenu-nefru*) was often employed on engineering and construction tasks. Montuhotep IV (1,998–1,991 BC) despatched 10,000 troops to Wadi Hammamat in order to transport a large block of stone for his burial sarcophagus back to the capital. On a smaller scale, from the tomb of Djehutihotep at el-Bersha comes a scene of a colossal statue being hauled into place by 172 men, organised in rows of four. The inscription accompanying the wall painting identifies the second row of men as soldiers. Pyramids continued to be built during the Middle Kingdom, and it is likely that conscript soldiers played a part in their construction too.

All troops went barefoot and, for many, their only protection was the common linen kilt worn by Egyptian commoners everywhere. Egyptian troops from this period are rarely depicted wearing any sort of armour, but occasionally a soldier is shown with white textile bands crossing his chest and shoulders. This may represent some kind of armour that was probably derived from Mesopotamian practice. Since these garments are typically illustrated in white, they are most likely formed from stiffened layers of linen, but they may just as easily be made up of leather. Greek hoplites, formidable warriors fighting across the Mediterranean centuries later, routinely protected themselves with a heavy cuirass of layered linen, providing a useful comparison to these Middle Kingdom Egyptians. On tomb paintings at el-Bersha, examples of leather or metal chest plates can be seen fastened beneath the linen bands. Helmets were not worn by Egyptian soldiers of the Middle Kingdom.

For those soldiers trained as 'shooters' (*megau*), their weaponry consisted of a simple stave bow and a handful of arrows. Quivers of leather or woven reeds are known from this period, but were not always in use and, instead, archers are often depicted clutching a handful of arrows. The *megau* might also carry a dagger or hand-axe as a secondary weapon. Archery dominated Egyptian warfare and the bow served Egypt as a symbol both of warfare and of royal power. Archers are depicted on a number of tomb paintings of the Middle Kingdom participating in ceremonies and processions.

Soldiers given hand-to-hand training were known as 'strong-arm fighters' (*nakhtu-aa*) and would instead be trained to fight with either a copper spear or hand-axe, in combination with a cowhide shield. Spears were often leaf-shaped and varied in length, although the spears carried by the model warriors in the tomb of Mesehti are, proportionately, 1.5 metres in length. Javelins were a specialised throwing spear, light in weight and short in length; depictions of them are common and they could be found in the hands of soldiers, hunters, doorkeepers, guards, and the soldiers assigned to riverboats. Javelins were stored in large leather quivers that were cylindrical in shape.

Axe-heads were lashed to their wooden hafts and were constructed in one of three styles: the splayed axe, the D-shaped axe, and the crescent-shaped epsilon axe. The latter took the form of a wide, curved blade, perforated by two holes and was a copy of a Syrian or Palestinian original. Its long cutting edge was perfect for inflicting maximum damage against unprotected targets. Unlike axes of today, which are mounted onto the wooden haft with a socket, early Egyptian axes were usually fitted into a slot in the side of the haft; holes drilled through the blade parallel with the haft were used to lash the blade firmly onto its handle using leather or sinew.

The wooden shields were large, up to 1.5 metres in height, flat along the bottom edge, and tapered to a curve or a point at the top; some of these are termed 'body shields' since they are tall enough to completely protect the user. Short, double-edged daggers would also have been carried into battle by troops and used by them in close-quarter fighting, or to despatch a wounded enemy. Copper was the most common metal used in the construction of these weapons and was inferior to the much harder bronze, used by some of Egypt's neighbours. During the Middle Kingdom, however, some readymade bronze items began to be imported from Palestine and Syria, although copper continued in use with Egyptian armourers.

Pharaoh Montuhotep II and his descendants formed the Eleventh Dynasty of Egypt and the stability and centralisation that they achieved continued into the Twelfth, a dynasty that was to last for two centuries. During this period, the capital was moved from Thebes, much further north, to Itj-tawy (modern el-Lisht) some 32 km south of the Old Kingdom capital Memphis. After 1,780 BC, the chronology of kings and events is poorly known, with many kings known only from fragmentary inscriptions. Disorder and confusion returned to Egypt, and scholars cannot agree on the exact number of Thirteenth Dynasty pharaohs—there may have been as few as ten and as many as seventy. Changing climatic conditions seem to have afflicted Egypt once again, with floods and droughts crippling both the economy and the social order of Egypt. Royal prestige may have suffered as a consequence of these hard times—the pharaoh could exercise no power over the fickle elements. This lack of confidence in the kingship explains the long line of pharaohs ruling in obscurity throughout the Thirteenth and Fourteenth Dynasties, few reigning long enough to erect monuments or memorials.

Within only a few decades of the start of the Thirteenth Dynasty, a breakaway line of kings (the Fourteenth Dynasty) set themselves up in the eastern Delta, presaging a catastrophic collapse in royal authority. As another Second Intermediate Period approached, a third line of kings emerged, reigning throughout the eastern Delta. These kings were foreign-born, Semitic immigrants from Palestine or Syria, and their rule over Lower Egypt is known as the Fifteenth Dynasty, although for the Egyptians of the day, it was a savage and unprecedented invasion by a barbarian peoples. The shock of foreign rule, after fifteen centuries of self-government, would sear itself into the psyche of all Egyptians, and both the nation and its fighting forces would be changed forever.

2

Invasion

Woe to the vanquished

Livy V.48

In the future, Egypt was to create a sophisticated, powerful, and well-equipped military force with which it dominated the Near East. This New Kingdom army would perfect the art of war. Yet such an effective and highly motivated military system would not spring magically from the subconscious of pharaoh. Egypt's military revolution, like so many others, would be driven by both a sense of humiliation and of survival.

Republican Rome famously suffered a number of invasions that scarred its psyche and kick-started energetic campaigns of military development. The first involved a powerful Celtic tribe called the Senones that had sacked Rome in 390 BC after defeating the army sent out to protect it. The second saw Rome outmatched and outnumbered by Carthaginian warships—but after capturing a stranded enemy ship during the First Punic War, the Romans ingeniously copied the design and built their first fleet within just sixty days. Finally, Hannibal, the brilliant Carthaginian general, marched an army into Italy and brought great pressure to bear on Rome and its beleaguered legions during the Second Punic War. Each of these defeats and reverses taught Rome a powerful lesson and helped forge the legions into the professional, disciplined, and determined fighting force that eventually conquered most of Western Europe.

The Princes of the Desert

Egypt's moment of greatest humiliation was to be the invasion of the kingdom by foreign invaders from Asia *circa* 1,650 BC. The origin of these mysterious usurpers is not known for certain, but the Egyptians referred to them as *hikau khasut* or

'Princes of the Desert Uplands'. The High Priest of Heliopolis, Manetho, writing later in the third century BC, wrongly translated this as 'Hyksos' or 'Shepherd Kings'—a term that has stuck ever since. Names of individual rulers are Semitic, suggesting that this wave of immigrants came from Palestine or Syria. The horror of the event, imprinted on the minds of Egyptians, was retold by priests many centuries after the event, and graphically recorded by the high priest Manetho:

> A blast of God smote us; and unexpectedly, from the regions of the East, invaders of obscure race marched in confidence of victory against our land. By main force they easily seized it without striking a blow; and having overpowered the rulers of the land, they then burned our cities ruthlessly, razed to the ground the temples of the gods....
>
> Aegyptiaca of Manetho

Manetho's striking account may reflect actual events, but it certainly does not tell us the whole story. The Thirteenth Dynasty of Egypt did not simply fall to a lightning attack of Semitic Syrian and Palestinian warlords that emerged from over the horizon ('they easily seized [Egypt] without striking a blow' according to the Aegyptiaca of Manetho). Immigrants from the Levant had been moving into Lower Egypt for more than a century before the take-over. Therefore, by the end of the Thirteenth Dynasty, the population of the Delta (particularly the eastern Delta) contained a mix of both native Egyptians and immigrant Semitic folk. A tomb painting from Beni Hasan depicts a group of these *hikau khasut* being received by an Egyptian nomarch during the reign of Seostris II (*c.* 1,880 BC) in the middle of the Twelfth Dynasty. The men of the tribe are armed with spears, throw sticks, and bows and they wear vividly coloured and patterned robes that bring to mind the story of Joseph and his coat of many colours. This familiar Old Testament tale records the travails of Palestinian shepherds who sojourned to Egypt during a time of hardship and famine. The Egyptian *Prophecy of Neferti* refers to an age-old tradition whereby desert Bedouin came to water their flocks among the reed swamps of eastern Egypt. They bought corn, traded goods, sought sanctuary, and (as the story of Joseph teaches us) sold one another into slavery. Over the course of a century, these settlers from Syria and Palestine had swollen the population of the eastern Delta immensely, earning a living as craftsmen, servants, and merchants. Some idea of their number can be gauged from the household of a Middle Kingdom official that contained no fewer than forty-five Semitic servants. Integration is difficult to imagine, Egyptian disdain from the Semitic folk is obvious from the names they employed for them: 'sand-dwellers, 'wretched foe', and 'vile' or 'miserable' Asiatics.

Of course, migration like this has occurred throughout history, and it is easy to see the attractions of Egypt to the desert nomads of the Near East—it was a paradise of food, water, civilisation and luxury. A steady flow of immigrants, albeit seasonal, might at times increase to a torrent during periods of severe drought. The collapse of once powerful Semitic states could also spur mass migration; throughout the eighteenth century BC, several Semitic dynasties were crushed or driven out of city-states like Kurda, Apum, and Mari, as well as the kingdoms of Sealand and Assyria.

Around 1,650 BC, the eastern Delta fell into the hands of a Semitic king, and we have only Manetho's account of that event to enlighten us. This may well have been some kind of peaceful transition during a time of crisis, during which the Thirteenth Dynasty was struggling to cope. Semitic communities forced to defend themselves against continued immigrant pressure would have backed their own war leader. During the chaos that prevailed at the end of the Thirteenth Dynasty, did the Semites invite such sympathetic warlords into the Delta to protect their communities?

However it came about, the eastern Delta and the city of Avaris fell to a Semitic dynasty of aggressive warlike kings. Pharaoh Mereneferre Ay failed to defend the capital city, and with the fall of Itj-tawy, the Thirteenth Dynasty came to an ignominious end. Mereneferre Ay was the last pharaoh of the dynasty to have his name recorded outside of Upper Egypt, which suggests the Egyptian government retreated south to Thebes. There may perhaps have been one final pharaoh of the Thirteenth Dynasty, Sekhemre Sankhtawy, who ruled from Memphis in Lower Egypt, but the stelae upon which this is based is of uncertain origin and cannot be trusted.

Pushed south to Thebes, the Egyptian pharaohs were forced to rule a greatly reduced kingdom along the valley of the Nile from Aswan to Abydos. The rich and populous estates of the Delta were lost to them. Cylinder seals of the first Hyksos king, Sheshi, have been found at the Nubian capital of Kush, a kingdom that dominated the Nile valley south of Aswan. The presence of this diplomatic seal can mean only one thing—that the Hyksos kings in the north had formed an alliance with the Nubians of the south. The Second Stele of Kamose, describing a military campaign against the Hyksos, explicitly mentions such an alliance. The surviving Egyptian dynasty was now boxed in, trapped without allies or access to resources.

For some time, this dynasty in exile lived under an uneasy truce with the Semitic kingdoms of Lower Egypt. Dynasties Fifteen and Sixteen were both Hyksos kingdoms, ruling the western and eastern halves of the Delta roughly contemporaneously with the remnants of Egyptian government at Thebes. The Theban line of kings is known as the Seventeenth Dynasty and it was essentially preserving the culture of the Middle Kingdom. Far from waging war against the foreign usurpers, it seems (from analysis of the etymology of the names of princesses of this period) that the pharaohs may initially have sanctioned intermarriage between the opposing royal houses—the traditional method of securing peace between mutually antagonistic states.

Peace was not to last, Egyptians regarded foreign rule as a terrible and shameful event. After a century of foreign domination and emboldened by the new military technology that the Hyksos had introduced and with which may they had defeated the Egyptians in battle, the Theban regime began a war of liberation. Slightly later, New Kingdom texts, such as the *Papyrus Sallier I* (from about 1,220 BC), suggest that the Hyksos period was viewed by Egyptians as nothing less than violent and ruthless domination of Egyptian culture by foreign warlords. The yoke of oppression had to be thrown off.

Perhaps then it was lucky that the Semitic kings had not followed up on their military victories by marching south to capture Thebes, thus ending the rule of Egyptian pharaohs for good. Yet the Hyksos remained in the Delta and they were part of a Near Eastern Bronze Age world from which the Middle Kingdom Egyptians had completely isolated themselves. Hyksos strongholds at their capital, Avaris, as well as Naytahut and Tjeku (modern Tell el-Dab'a, el-Yahudiyeh and el-Maskhuta respectively), have revealed archaeological evidence of the Semitic culture of the Hyksos invaders. Large amounts of Syro-Palestine pottery and other material have been found at these and other Delta sites, dated, in Near Eastern chronologies, to the Middle Bronze Age II Period (*c.* 2,000–1,700 BC). Some of the new kings aped the royal titular and seem to have supported and perpetuated an Egyptian form of government. Egyptian gods were both recognised and worshipped, but new Syrian gods were also introduced, deities such as Reshef, Anat, and Astarte became thoroughly integrated into the native pantheon. Trade links were maintained with sites like Byblos and Crete, and they were extended. Lower Egypt was now plugged into a Bronze Age trading network and it would never be the same again.

By around 1,650 BC, the Hyksos had appointed an overall war leader, Sheshi, the first pharaoh of the Fifteenth Dynasty. Sheshi was later succeeded by Yakubher and then Khyan, who promoted trade abroad from his base at Avaris. The next Hyksos chieftain, Apophis, adopted an Egyptian personal name and it was during his long forty-year reign that conflict eventually erupted between the Hyksos state in Lower Egypt and the surviving Egyptian dynasty.

How had Egypt been brought so low? The natural barriers that had previously protected the kingdom from invasion had insulated it from the outside world, not just socially and politically, but also technologically. While the armies of the Hurrian and Semitic city-states had adopted horse-drawn chariots, bronze weapon technology, and composite war bows in a feverish arms race with one another, the Egyptians were unaware that there even was an arms race. Their levy troops, barefooted and unarmoured, had been up to the task of quelling Nubian rebels or defeating Semitic or Libyan shepherds on the desert fringes, but technologically, they were no better equipped than the simple tribes that they marched out to defeat. Basic stave bows, copper axes, and copper-headed spears were used by both Egyptian soldiers and their foes. The Middle Kingdom army had enjoyed an advantage only in numbers and in the sophisticated organisation brought about by highly literate and well-trained scribes.

Military Innovation

Hyksos chiefs were not simply opportunistic Bedouin who led their tribes into an Egypt that was falling apart, they were war leaders. For example, 50 per cent of the male Hyksos graves that were excavated at Tell el Dab'a contained a weapon—80 per cent of these axes, daggers, and spears were of Syro-Palestinian origin, indicating that they brought their tools, weapons and fighting styles with them from the East. Asiatic-style axes had already been introduced to Egypt during the Middle Kingdom, but the Hyksos did bring with them the distinctive *khopesh*. Resembling outwardly a reaping sickle used by farmers for harvesting crops, the *khopesh* was actually more of a scimitar, it was the outer curved edge that formed the sharpened killing blade. Hyksos archers were equipped with a composite bow, formed from several layers of wood, horn, and glue that proved far more powerful than the simple wooden self bows used by the native Egyptian army. Composite bows were neither a Hyksos, Syrian, nor Palestinian innovation, but were first used by Akkadian troops in Mesopotamia, 700 years earlier. This fact just goes to emphasise the large gulf that existed between Egyptian military technology and that of its Near Eastern neighbours.

Horse-drawn chariots were certainly known to the Syrian city-states at this time. Unfortunately, there are no depictions of Hyksos warriors or the chariots that they introduced. It is likely that the so-called Florence chariot that was recovered in pieces from an unknown Egyptian tomb (and is currently held in the Egyptian Museum of Florence) represents the earliest example of an Egyptian chariot and must closely resemble the Hyksos originals. The Florence chariot features a simple light-weight frame and four-spoked wheels. Identical chariots do appear on cylinder seal impressions from Nuzi, a city-state in Mesopotamia, of approximately the same date. By the time of Tutankhamun's death in 1,323 BC, six-spoked wheels had been adopted by chariot-makers across the ancient world.

Chariots of and by themselves do not revolutionise warfare, the Hyksos brought with them a 'tactical package' of military equipment and fighting styles that changed the way that the Egyptians would wage war in the future. Although the first war chariots were developed in ancient Sumeria, they did not achieve their greatest tactical potential until the rise of various Hurrian states in northern Syria. Hurrian chariot warriors (*maryannu*) mastered the skills of both horsemanship and chariot warfare and formed an aristocratic elite that proved the cream of the army. In essence, they became the knights and chevaliers of their day. A Hurrian manual of arms was written by one Kikkuli and it survived within the tablet house of ancient Hattusas. It illustrates how horses were carefully selected and bred and how they were trained, exercised, and graded.

Hurrian armies realigned themselves around their core striking force, the chariotry, with infantry serving almost as an auxiliary arm. The 'punch' of this *maryannu* chariotry came not from the speed or power of the horses themselves, but from the warriors that the chariots carried. Each chariot acted as a fast-moving 'weapons platform'. Part and parcel of the chariot system was the adoption of long armour coats by the *maryannu*, coats that were made up of hundreds of bronze scales. Bronze helmets and powerful composite bows completed this 'package'. While his driver kept the horses at a gallop and just within bow range of the enemy, the *maryannu* used his composite bow to rain down arrows upon his foe. Clay tablets that record the organisation and maintenance of these chariot units indicate that they could operate in very large formations, some containing more than 100 individual chariot teams. The effect of dozens of these fast-moving and unassailable attackers sweeping around an army's flanks and peppering it with deadly arrows must have been shocking.

A War of Liberation

The fight back began under the reign of Egyptian Pharaoh Seqenenre Tao, who waged a diplomatic war of words with the Hyksos leader Apophis. Little else is known of Seqenenre's reign, which is a pity, since his mummy was discovered in 1881 and shows clear signs of a violent death. During an autopsy performed on the body in the 1970s, deep gashes to his head were matched with Palestinian-style axe-heads. The attack had been ferocious and the weight of forensic evidence suggests that Seqenenre Tao died while waging war on the Hyksos. Gaston Maspero, the French Egyptologist, discovered the murdered pharaoh's mummy in a cache along with dozens of others. He described the injuries in detail:

> The appearance of his mummy proves that he died a violent death when about forty years of age. Two or three men, whether assassins or soldiers, must have surrounded and despatched him before help was available. A blow from an axe must have severed part of his left cheek, exposed the teeth, fractured the jaw, and sent him senseless to the ground; another blow must have seriously injured the skull, and a dagger or javelin has cut open the forehead on the right side, a little above the eye. His body must have remained lying where it fell for some time: when found, decomposition had set in, and the embalming had to be hastily performed as best it might. The hair is thick, rough, and matted; the face had been shaved on the morning of his death, but by touching the cheek we can ascertain how harsh and abundant the hair must have been. The

> mummy is that of a fine, vigorous man, who might have lived to a hundred years, and he must have defended himself resolutely against his assailants; his features bear even now an expression of fury. A flattened patch of exuded brain appears above one eye, the forehead is wrinkled, and the lips, which are drawn back in a circle about the gums, reveal the teeth still biting into the tongue.
>
> Gaston Maspero
> *History of Egypt, Chaldæa, Syria, Babylonia, and Assyria*, Volume 4

Contrary to Maspero's beliefs, however, there were no defensive wounds found on the arms of Seqenenre Tao. The body showed signs of decomposition as if it had lain abandoned for a time and the mummification procedure (when it was begun) was shoddily completed, with eyes and brain matter still *in situ*. This evidence and the findings of more recent tests have suggested that the king was probably despatched in the style of an execution, perhaps in the presence of the Hyksos king or even by his hand.

It was Seqenenre's son, Kamose, who began to claw back Egyptian territory from the Hyksos and their Nubian allies. An account unearthed at Karnak on two important stelae recounts Kamose's third regnal year, which aptly captures the frustration felt by the Egyptians of Thebes:

> To what end am I cognisant of it, this power of mine, when a chieftain is in Avaris and another in Kush, and I sit in league with an Aamu and a Nubian, every man holding his slice of this Egypt.
>
> The Second Stelae of Kamose

After sailing downstream, Kamose led his army in an attack on the stronghold of Teti, a local governor and Hyksos collaborator near Hermopolis. This victory caused panic and uproar within the enemy's capital at Avaris, and the Hyksos king retreated behind the city's fortifications. Unable or unwilling to besiege the Avaris, Kamose returned south to proclaim the campaign a victory. In addition, he struck out in other directions; troops were despatched to the Bahriya Oasis in order to sever communications between Nubia and Avaris, and Lower Nubia was occupied by force. If the Hyksos kings thought that Kamose's death in 1,550 BC would grant some kind of reprieve, they were wrong—his son, Ahmose I, continued his father's work, resuming the military campaign halfway through his twenty-four year reign. Our only contemporary account of this momentous campaign comes not from the boasts of the pharaoh himself, carved upon some temple wall, but from the war diary of one of the king's officers. Also named Ahmose, this nobleman served in the pharaoh's naval task force and his achievements were recorded within his private tomb at el-Kab, just to the north of Aswan. Ahmose, son of Ebana, followed his pharaoh, King Ahmose I, into battle many times. He fought at the siege of Avaris, as well as at the second and third battles of Avaris. He was there at the city's eventual capture and he joined the army on its expedition out of Egypt to strike at Hyksos base areas in Palestine. Ahmose also participated in the six-year-long siege of Sharuhen, which seems to have been a rallying point for the fleeing Hyksos forces. Once the army returned, it was despatched immediately to Nubia, before being recalled back to Egypt once more in order to quell two successive rebellions.

Accounts like that of Ahmose son of Ebana are rare in ancient history. One would think that a literate society (such as ancient Rome) would provide many examples of military diary, but there are precious few, the most notable being that of Ammianus Marcellenus, a junior cavalry officer from the fourth century AD. Accounts of people's lives in ancient Egypt are even rarer, which makes Ahmose's words extremely valuable. Most of Egyptian military history comes from the self-aggrandisement of a pharaoh's own victory celebrations, the carvings proclaiming his achievements on the temple walls. Rarely do we have eyewitness statements. Ahmose tells us of each battle in which he participated; that he took human hands (the standard battle trophy, marking a single 'kill'), that he was awarded gold for his efforts, that he later took captives, and was awarded both slaves and gold for his bravery:

> I served as an officer in (my father's) stead, in the ship The Offering in the time of the Lord of the Two Lands, Ahmose I, triumphant while I was still young, not having taken a wife.
>
> Biography of Ahmose, son of Ebana

Ahmose then described his achievements during the campaign against the Hyksos stronghold:

> One besieged the city of Avaris; I showed valor on foot before his majesty; then I was appointed to (the ship) Shining-in-Memphis... one fought on the water in the canal, Pezedku of Avaris. Then I fought hand to hand, I brought away a hand (as a trophy)... Then there was again fighting in this place; I again fought hand to hand... one captured Avaris; I took captive there one man and three women, total four heads, his majesty gave them to me for slaves.
>
> Biography of Ahmose, son of Ebana

After more than a century of foreign occupation, Ahmose I, pharaoh of Egypt, had expelled the Hyksos from the Delta and restored the southern boundary of Egypt with Nubia in the south. Ahmose became the first king of a new resurgent

Egyptian dynasty, the Eighteenth, and he led the kingdom into a new and self-confident age of expansion and dynamism. Egyptologists refers to this new age of military confidence as the New Kingdom.

We should ask how the Egyptian army managed to drive out the Hyksos in *circa* 1,540 BC when it was forced to relinquish the Delta to the Semitic foe a century earlier. Egyptologists generally agree that significant innovations in military technology and organisation took place during the Seventeenth Dynasty, no doubt inspired by, and copied from, the Hyksos. The city-states of Syria and Palestine had gained an impressive military lead on Egypt, something that the Egyptian kings were forced to rectify. First, the army had to be modernised if Egypt was to stand any hope of facing the Hyksos on the battlefield, and second, the Semitic kingdoms of the Near East must be prevented from ever regaining the initiative again. Egyptian tactics and technology were both transformed in the wake of the Hyksos take-over, but perhaps the greatest change would be in a shift of strategic thinking. Ahmose I, in his seven-year siege of Sharuhen, was clearly sending out a message to the Semitic kings: Egypt would no longer sit complacently behind its frontiers; instead, it would push out into the world and dominate its neighbours. Attack would become the primary defence of the New Kingdom.

Ahmose, son of Ebana, the naval officer who fought in the campaign of liberation, was at pains to stress his naval service, since the fleet had always formed the heart of the Middle Kingdom war machine. Each ship captain was directly responsible to the pharaoh, bringing the navy and its personnel great prestige. The Nile formed the focus of communication and travel within Egypt, and so warfare and the strategic thinking behind it was primarily water based. Ordinary foot soldiers were inferior to the sailors, who were part of an elite 'senior service'. Tactics, therefore, had never called for chariots and horses, since troops were moved quickly by water to trouble spots along the Nile; additionally, the populated areas lacked the wide open spaces required for chariot warfare. For Middle Kingdom military commanders, this reliance on the ships and marines of the Egyptian navy meant that foreign lands some distance from the Nile were always difficult to effectively annex.

Pharaoh Ahmose's siege of Avaris displays the limitations imposed on the Egyptian army by the natural geography of the Nile Delta. The city sat on a river channel, surrounded by reed beds and marshland that forced the pharaoh to rely on his navy to make the initial attack. Fragments of a battle relief from Ahmose's pyramid temple at Abydos shine some light on the forces employed by Ahmose in his war on the Hyksos. A royal ship is depicted, representing the role of the Egyptian navy, there are archers, loosing arrows high into the air; another fragment of the relief depicts a team of chariot horses. With his enemy hiding behind the walls of Avaris, though, this new wheeled-weapon must have played only a small part in the liberation of the Delta. It seems, then, from these tantalising pieces of the relief, that the Hyksos were routed by a combination of tried and tested Egyptian naval tactics, coupled with the new weapon of warfare, the horse and chariot.

A century of exile at Thebes had been used to imitate the construction and use of chariots along with Semitic-style, narrow-bladed axes and powerful composite bows. Horses were also needed in large quantities, and we know that the established custom was to capture enemy horses following a battlefield victory. Ahmose's father, Kamose, boasts on one relief that he 'will take over chariotry' as he sets out to vanquish the Hyksos. Many of the Seventeenth Dynasty's horses may have been acquired in this way, with the remainder being imported from Syria during intervals of peace.

With the task of liberation complete, Egypt remade itself. The next phase of Egyptian history is known today as the New Kingdom—a radical rebirth of the ancient kingdom. The state now lauded its military forces and embraced military imagery, carving their deeds and victories onto the kingdom's grandest monuments. The office of pharaoh began to encompass the role of war leader, protected from harm and guided in battle by Amun, a minor god that was on the ascendency. Amun had been the local god of Thebes during the exile of the Egyptian royal court. He had proved a powerful psychological lever for the growing fight-back, a rallying point and a source of hope. New Kingdom pharaohs could point to Amun's divine intervention during the successful expulsion of the Hyksos warlords from Egypt. In the future, both the city of Thebes and its obscure god would play a major part in the development of this New Kingdom.

3

The New Kingdom Army

Utterance of Amon: 'Take to thyself the sword, O mighty king, Horus of the bows, in order to overthrow the wretched chiefs of Kush, in order to cut off their heads. Thy terror enters into their bodies, like Sekhmet when she rages'.

Inscription from Redesiyeh

Following its victory over the Hyksos, the Egyptian army became a permanent major institution, funded, recruited, and maintained by the Egyptian state. The pharaoh stood at its head, and although he did not always accompany the army into battle, it became increasingly more common for him to do so. Temple inscriptions describe the almost superhuman prowess and fighting ability of the king, yet in reality he was always accompanied (and protected) by a guard of elite chariot troops as well as top officials, military commanders, and even royal princes. Ramses II also possessed two units of elite royal infantrymen, one composed of native Egyptians and the other formed from captive *Shardana* warriors.

Divisions

According to an edict of Horemheb (1,319–1,307 BC), Egypt was initially defended by two army divisions (*mesha*)—one garrisoned the north of the country, while the other guarded the south. Later, a third division was created and Tuthmosis III (1,479–1,425 BC) took these three army corps, named Amun, Re, and Ptah, with him to fight the Mitanni at the Battle of Megiddo. The divisions were named after the patron gods of the territories from which they were recruited and in which they were based: Amun at Thebes, Re at Heliopolis, and Ptah at Memphis. In this way, the new military administration mirrored the civil administration. Each division came under the command of a senior

Officers of the Egyptian army, each carrying a standard as a badge of rank. The leader of the group is a son of the pharaoh and wears body armour.

commander who was responsible for recruiting fresh troops, for the supply and provisioning of the military units, and for the provision of royal escorts. The complex logistics that this entailed was supervised by the King's Scribe of Recruits as well as the Chief Scribes of the Army; beneath these officials worked an army of military scribes, operating at every level. Like the Roman legions that came after it, the army of New Kingdom Egypt maintained comprehensive and up-to-date records, contributing to its efficiency and effectiveness.

When Ramses II (1,290–1,224 BC) moved the capital to a new city in the Delta called Piramesse, he created a fourth division with which to garrison it. This latest army corps was named Set and it marched into Syria along with the Ra, Ptah, and Amun divisions when Ramses II met the Hittites at the battle of Kadesh.

Egyptian records do not give us the number of troops within a single division, but modern estimates range from 1,000 to 5,000, with the larger figure probably a more viable estimate. A satirical account by the scribe Hori from the

Papyrus Anastasi I describes how a force of 5,000 soldiers might be provisioned, lending weight to the figure of 5,000 for a division. Adding further weight to this figure is the Hammamat Stela, which records a quarrying expedition that was despatched by Pharaoh Ramses IV (1,163–1,156 BC) out to the Wadi Hammamat, which included 2,000 temple staff, hundreds of stonemasons, as well as 5,000 infantrymen.

In the same way that a Roman legion or a modern US infantry division is a self-contained military force, the Egyptian *mesha* could also operate independently in the field. On campaign, these divisions might be separated from one another by distances of over 10 km, but by remaining in constant contact via riders or chariots, they always retained the ability to support one another. In an age where enemy chariot forces sought to outflank, cut off, and harry the Egyptian units, this tactic of close co-operation and support served an important role.

The Infantry

The Hammamat Stela was not a serious military document but rather a scribe's stinging attack on one of his comrades, yet it does place twenty infantry commanders on the expedition, under an overall commandant of the army. This suggests that each division of 5,000 soldiers was actually composed of twenty sub-units, each one made up of 250 men. Companies (or *sa*) of this size are attested elsewhere and each of these *sa* had its own commander and battle standard. Since there are twenty military scribes also listed in the Hammamat Stela, it would seem as if each *sa* also retained its own scribe who would be responsible for maintaining the company's records. It seems to have been the standard-bearer (*tjai-seryt*) who was in command of the Egyptian company, and he was assisted by three junior officers: a military scribe, a deputy (*idnu*), and a quartermaster. Five officers, called the 'Greatest of Fifty', also reported to the company commander. Perhaps the 250 men of the *sa* was a theoretical maximum, but it was often maintained at much lower levels due to lack of manpower, casualties, sickness, or some tactical requirement.

Soldiers within the company were subdivided into platoons of fifty, each of which was commanded by one of the 'Greatest of Fifty'. At the bottom of the organisational rung were the individual infantry squads, familiar to every army, both past and present. Egyptian infantry squads were comprised of ten men and therefore there must have been five squads to a platoon. Individual soldiers must have felt great loyalty to their company, they would have rallied to its standard and taken pride in its history. Many names and titles of Egyptian *sa* have been preserved, including, for example, 'Beloved of Amun', 'Bull in Nubia', 'Aton is Resplendent', and 'Menkheprure—Destroyer of Syria'. In reliefs that depict these units, the 'Greatest of Fifty' and 'Greatest of Ten' (similar to modern NCOs) were dressed in the manner of their troops, but carried wooden staves or batons with which to berate their men.

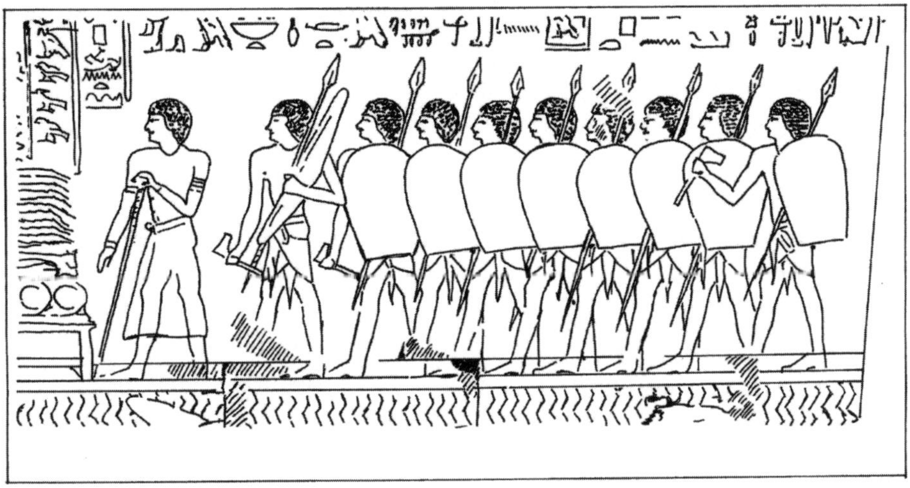

Spearmen of Queen Hatshepsut's army march behind their unit commander. Each man holds a round-topped shield and spear in his left hand, and a battle-axe in his right. Note the soldier to the rear of the officer who carries a bow case.

A fighting force, operating as a tactical unit on the battlefield, may have been an individual company, or two or more companies acting in unison. These battlefield formations were known as a host (or *pedjet*). A host would have its own commander as well as additional troops and attached officers, including an assault officer and transport officer. War trumpets were used to communicate orders and examples of such trumpets have been found within tombs.

Infantry troops were of two main types, the archers (*megau*, literally 'shooters') and the hand-to-hand soldiers (*nakhtu-aa*, literally 'strong-arm fighters'). The archers were equipped with either the simple stave bow of the Middle Kingdom, or, more increasingly, with the composite bow of which there were several different designs. Archers could provide covering fire for the hand-to-hand warriors, softening up a target before the troops met in melee combat. Against unarmoured foes, such as Nubian or Libyan tribesmen, the archers themselves proved to be an effective combat force, easily able to drive back or decimate a foe with a massed volley of arrows. The partially mummified remains of the Deir el-Bahri soldiers illustrate this all too well.

'Strong-arm fighters' are depicted on temple walls either engaged in one-on-one combat, stabbing with a spear, hacking at a foe with an axe or sword, or arrayed in a battle-line, with shields locked together. It is clear that the Egyptian foot soldier could fight effectively in either manner, as the opponent, terrain, or situation dictated. Spears were carried by the strong-arm fighters, which they either threw at the enemy before closing with them or used in combination with the shield-wall formation in order to fight defensively from behind the safety of that shield barrier. All carried additional weaponry, typically an axe or club, but sometimes instead the *khopesh*, the curved scimitar-like sword that had been introduced into Egypt by the Hyksos. Weapons were now of bronze, rather than the softer metal copper. Both archers and spearmen had a role to play in siege warfare; the fighters are shown conducting sapper operations on enemy fortifications, while the archers protect them with volleys of arrows aimed up at the battlements of the city under siege. Archers and frontline fighters were not mixed with a single company, but were probably brigaded separately—each troop type within its own *sa*.

The Chariotry

The crew of an Egyptian chariot comprised of an armoured warrior of some status, as well as a chariot-driver who doubled as a shield-bearer. In Egyptian texts, he is called either a *kedjen* ('charioteer') or sometimes a *ger'iu* ('shield-bearer'). Weaponry carried by the warrior (*seneny*) included a composite bow, one or more quivers of arrows, several bronze-bladed javelins, and a *khopesh* or mace. In a way, one could compare the Bronze Age chariot to the tank of the First World War, a weapons platform that was primarily designed to completely overwhelm the traditional infantry unit. Churchill's tracked tanks relied on armour plate for their invulnerability, while the Egyptian chariots relied on sheer speed and manoeuvrability.

Each chariot formed a self-contained combat unit that included a third crewman, a runner, who was attached to the chariot and who either ran alongside it or hitched a lift. The runner (*peherer*) fought in support of his chariot and must have been specially selected for his speed and endurance. Runners are depicted moving ahead of the chariots, or to the rear, mopping up the enemy following a chariot charge. They are typically shown unarmoured, carrying light shields and javelins. Although a small number appear to be archers, it is unclear whether these men are *peherer* armed with bows or simply chariot-warriors from destroyed vehicles who are fighting on foot.

Ten chariots formed a single troop, commanded by a 'first charioteer' (*kedjen-tepy*) and five of these chariot troops were organised as a fifty-chariot squadron led by a 'Standard Bearer of the Chariot Warriors'; Pharaoh Merenptah (1,224–1,214 BC)—one of the sons of Ramses I ('the Great')—records how, as a prince, he served in two different chariot squadrons named 'The Phoenix' and 'Manifest-in-Justice'. Like the infantry company (*sa*), the chariot squadron had a number of officers attached to it, as reliefs at Abu Simbel show. The reliefs illustrating Ramses the Great's military camp at Kadesh depict a stable-master and an adjutant, as well as a number of grooms, scribes, and craftsmen. The existence of these support personnel at the squadron level indicate that it acted as the primary tactical unit in any chariot deployment. Chariot teams would return to the squadron to repair their vehicles, stable their horses, and rearm. In the same way that infantry companies combined to form a war host (*pedjet*), chariot squadrons could come together to form their own hosts, each led by a 'Standard Bearer of

Mercenaries. These Sea Peoples fight for Egypt, yet they retain their Syrian-style kilts, round shields, and native helmets.

Chariot Warriors'. Hosts varied in size, depending on the number of squadrons that could be combined. It may have followed the same pattern as the infantry hosts and contained five squadrons, for a total of 250 vehicles.

Auxiliary Troops

Contingents of foreign troops were employed extensively during the New Kingdom. Some of these, principally troops from the cities of Palestine and Syria, fought as a feudal obligation to the Egyptian state that ruled their home territory. Others had been enslaved during wars of conquest and now served within the Egyptian army system, their fighting talent appreciated and harnessed rather than left to fester amid malcontent and rebellion. Peoples known to have entered service with the army in this way included Libyans, Nubians, Bedouin, and *Shardana* (a northern group of warriors with uncertain origins). Ramses the Great defeated and then recruited an entire unit of *Shardana* to serve as his guard and they are depicted on the walls of his great temple of Abu Simbel. These warriors look radically different from the native Egyptians, they wear horned helmets and body armour and carry both circular shields and longswords into battle. The helmet of each *Shardana* is topped by what appears to be a small sphere or a disc, emblematic of the sun.

The most famous of the Nubian auxiliaries were the Medjay; they were mainly archers and found employ as scouts and skirmishers from the Middle Kingdom onwards. Pharaoh Kamose is known to have used these troops in his struggle against the Hyksos. Medjay originated in the deserts to the east of the

Nile and within the region of Lower Nubia. During the last centuries of the New Kingdom, the unique cultural traits of the Medjay are no longer detected within their burials and they become almost indistinguishable from native Egyptians. The unit was maintained, however, and later tasked with patrolling the Valley of the Kings and the regions surrounding it. They had become a 'necropolis police', deterring tomb robbers from the burials of the pharaohs and their queens and princes. Like Egyptian foot soldiers, the Medjay fought in companies, each one led by an officer called a *hery-Medjay*, a 'Chief of Medjay', who commanded the entire formation with the assistance of a deputy (*idnu*).

Much like auxiliaries in other ancient armies, these foreign fighters were not fully integrated into the established infantry hierarchy, they fought in their native costume, with their traditional weapons, and this meant that they could perform unique roles on the battlefield. While the native Egyptian companies were either filled with massed archers or spearmen, auxiliary troops like the Nubian and Libyan tribesmen acted as skirmishers, able to harass enemy forces from a distance, scout ahead of the main force, and carry out ambush attacks. The *Shardana*, however, were more suited to frontline combat and we know that these northern warriors were some of Ramses II's best troops.

A mercenary from Canaan with his wife. He drinks beer from a jar through a reed pipe and is assisted by his Egyptian slave.

A clue to the status and luxury that a successful mercenary might look forward too is indicated on a painted limestone stele from the Eighteenth Dynasty city of Amarna. It shows a Syrian mercenary, sporting his customary (and very un-Egyptian) beard, seated on a decorated stool, his spear propped up behind him and his Syrian wife in attendance before him. An Egyptian slave is shown helping his master drink beer from a jug through a reed straw.

Elite Troops

Mention has already been made of the enigmatic *Shardana* who formed the core of Ramses' personal guard unit. Reliance on foreign fighters in this way continued through history, the early Caesars were protected by a cohort of German tribal warriors, the Byzantine emperors by the Viking warriors of the Varangian Guard, and the Catholic popes of Rome have relied on the famous Swiss Guard for their personal safety for over 500 years. The reasons are obvious: foreign-born mercenaries are outside of the normal social structure and so the *Shardana* would not easily have been embroiled in the court intrigues and dynastic struggles that plague powerful states like Rome, Byzantium, and ancient Egypt.

Beyond the pharaoh's personal guard, there appeared in the Eighteenth Dynasty a class of elite troops that could be relied on to lead the charge or the assault on a foreign city. They were known as the 'King's Braves' (*kenyt-nesu*) and their numbers were filled with distinguished soldiers from the rank and file of the infantry *sa* who had been promoted for their bravery on the battlefield.

Logistics

All armies require a large degree of logistical support and this means that they must be fed, transported, armed, and clothed. This in itself requires an administrative network and Egypt could boast a sophisticated hierarchy of scribes that served that very purpose. The New Kingdom army had its own 'militarised' scribes that were embedded at every level; they kept detailed records of enemy captives, booty that had been captured in battle, as well as the rations and supplies to be distributed among the troops. In addition, some of them acted as heralds (*wehenu*), conveying orders between commanders and their subordinates.

Egyptian victories on the battlefield resulted in the *wehenu* reported acts of bravery to the pharaoh, often resulting in promotion for the individual soldier or to an award of gold, slaves, or land. Victories also meant an enemy death toll that had to be counted. In order to encourage their troops to take lives and increase the overall body count, commanders usually awarded a bounty for every severed hand brought into camp. Wary of tempting the Egyptian soldier into mutilating the bodies of his fallen comrades, the practice was restricted to the dead of those foreign tribes that had darker complexions than the Egyptians. Libyan warriors, however, were of a similar skin colour to the native Egyptians, which led commanders fighting against the Libyans to instead offer up a bounty for every severed phallus, rather than a hand. Since Egyptians routinely circumcised their young boys and the Libyans did not, this served as an easily identifiable distinction. At Medinet Habu, Ramses III recorded a glorious victory over the Sea Peoples on his temple walls. In one scene, two piles of human body parts, one of severed phalli and the other of severed hands, illustrates perfectly the brutal practice of bounty payments.

Tjaunny was a military scribe from the New Kingdom, who had his career recorded on the walls of his tomb: 'he recorded the soldiers in the presence of his majesty, recorded those eligible for the elite troops, and instructed all men in their military duties'. While some scribes might be counting severed hands, others might have more exalted positions. When Tuthmosis III led an expedition into Syria to make war on the Mitanni, scribes were at his side to record not just the outcome of the battle, but also the decisions of his generals and even the words spoken in counsel by the pharaoh. Still others recorded the flora and fauna of the region through which they travelled; these findings were later reproduced on wall carvings within the 'Botanical Gardens' at the temple of Karnak.

The importance of military logistics proved to be far greater in the New Kingdom than in previous centuries. Now, liberated by the chariot and moving deeper than ever before into foreign territories, the army could no longer rely on supply ships sailing up and down the Nile for food and equipment. An open road, coupled with an efficient logistics train, was needed to keep New Kingdom soldiers active in Palestine and Syria for long periods of time. Donkeys, horses, and oxen are shown around Ramses II's camp at Kadesh, all of which may have served as draft animals. Oxen, however, are particularly slow (achieving a speed of around 3.2 kph), especially when compared to mules and donkeys (which are able to make upwards of 6.4 kph—comparable to a fast walk for a human). Although oxen are capable of hauling heavy carts filled with supplies, they have the disadvantage of working hard only for relatively short periods. While mules and donkeys can be pushed for up to eight hours or more, the ox must rest after only five. Ox carts are shown in use by some of Egypt's enemies, particularly the Sea Peoples, who were using them to transport their families across the Egyptian border. Based on the speed of some Egyptian marches, such as Tuthmosis III's trip from Sile in the Delta to Gaza (which made around 20 km per day), it is unlikely that oxen were used by the Egyptian army for transportation. The cattle at Kadesh may have been requisitioned from local people simply for their meat.

As a minimum, the food supplies required for a campaign in hot climes are:

Men	6.6 kg of grain (or equivalent)
	1.9 litres of water
Horses/Mules/Donkeys	22 kg of forage
	30 litres of water

These figures suggest that constant resupply would have been necessary when the army was on campaign; indeed, the royal inscriptions of victorious pharaohs often refer to numerous arrivals and departures from specific towns. Some of these would be held by allied princes who were treaty-bound to provide succour to the army of the pharaoh, while others were Egyptian supply posts. Arriving at these cities, the army would have camped outside of the walls where there was always ample space for tents and camp fires and where the horses and pack animals could be fed and watered.

Simply crossing from the Delta into Palestine forced the army to traverse the inhospitable Sinai Desert; for this, local water sources and pre-positioned supply dumps would have been a necessity. Rations were easy to carry, Alexander the Great's troops were able to carry up to ten days of food with them and the Roman legions always left their forts with at least three days' worth of hard-tack. Water, however, was another story. Waterskins were unreliable and limited in their capacity, while jars and amphorae were heavy and difficult to transport. Pharaoh and his advisors planned the route of the army by way of available water sources. Tuthmosis III, for example, led his army out of the Aruna Pass and directly to the Kina Brook where his troops and their animals could water. At allied cities, animals could be grazed on the surrounding farmland, while the troops would have needed the support of the inhabitants. Cities like Gaza provided grain, meat, and vegetables and served as crucial staging points for Egyptian campaigns into the north.

It is clear, however, that treks across the Sinai and through the inhospitable Aruna Pass would force any Egyptian army to carry rations with it on the march. These rations had to be dispersed among all the mobilised soldiers, a complex task that fell to the military scribes. Soldiers were entitled to fresh bread, wheat grains, ointment, and linen and could claim their allotment by handing over a wooden tally that was carved in the shape of a loaf to a scribe.

In the British Museum, a papyrus from the Twentieth Dynasty mentions the disbursement of military rations. However, the author was a government scribe, Wenmediamen, who was at pains to denigrate the life of a soldier—he provides a grim account of the infantryman's daily routine:

> He receives the corn-ration when he is released from [his] duty, but it is rotten when it is ground [on a mill-stone]. There are no clothes and no sandals, the weapons of warfare are at the fortress of Tjel. During his march he drinks water every three days—it tastes like salt. His body is crushed … his body is weakened and his legs are feeble.'
>
> *Papyrus Lansing*

An inscription from the time of Seti I describes an expedition of 1,000 soldiers that had been sent out to bring back sandstone for one of the pharaoh's building projects. It gives details of the daily ration awarded to each man in the unit and this included 1.82 kg of bread, vegetables (in bundles), and one piece of roast meat; in addition, two sacks (the meaning here is confused) of grain were awarded each month. Professor Anthony Spallinger has calculated that within Seti's expeditionary force, each man would have consumed around 4,175 calories. In comparison, the modern US Army calculates its Military Dietary Reference Intakes (MDRI) between 3,250 and 4,600 calories for a modern American male, 1.75 metres in height and weighing 79 kg. The typical Egyptian or Nubian soldier would certainly have been smaller and consumed less, yet the US Army's MDRI and the daily rations doled out by Seti's scribes provide an interesting point of comparison.

Military Standards

Large, well-organised armies require efficient methods of signalling and control, and the Egyptians achieved this through the use of both trumpets and drums as well as with battle standards. Drums provided a rhythmic beat that kept large units of soldiers marching together in unison. Trumpets are known to have been employed on the battlefield as a method of transmitting signals, although the commands must have been fairly general, such as 'advance', 'charge', or 'retreat'. Two bronze war trumpets were recovered from Tutankhamun's tomb, each with a wooden former that was inserted inside the body of the delicate instrument in order to protect it from damage when not in use. Troops are also known to have sung war hymns and used war cries as they marched into battle. One of these songs survives within the tomb of a Sixth Dynasty army officer called Unas.

Units identified themselves with unique military standards that seem to have been carried either by dedicated standard-bearers or the actual commanders themselves; remember that the *sa* was commanded by a *tjai-seryt* (which translates as 'standard-bearer'). Standard-bearers shown on the walls of the Temple of Hatshepsut at Deir el-Bahri are armed with bows, which certainly suggests they were combat capable troops. Each army division—Set, Ptah, Re, and Amun—had its own standard that represented the god of that unit, but troops within smaller units, like the company, also followed their own standard. One rectangular standard bearing the name of the god Aten appears in a tomb at Amarna; to one side is the hieroglyph for *sa*, denoting a military company. Men could rally around these insignia—they provided unit recognition and *esprit de corps*, in the same way that the modern British army regiments value their colours or the Roman legions revered their eagles. Red and white streamers hung from the Egyptian battle standards, these were the national colours of the kingdom and the colours of the two crowns (one of Upper and one of Lower Egypt).

Some battle standards were made up of dyed ostrich feathers and were set into a fan design. There are others of a rectangular shape that probably held the

Battle standards. Many military standards featured animal symbols, deities, and sun barques. Each unit had its own standard, carried into battle by the unit commander.

unit's name and titles. A number of other standards are depicted on reliefs and many show animals such as hawks, lions, and antelope, while others show more religious symbols. Single ostrich plume standards were carried by high-ranking chariot officers, and it is likely that these served as a rallying point for other chariots within the squadron.

Garrisons and Forts

Throughout the New Kingdom, Egypt was a place of relative peace and security, only on the borders with foreign nations or in zones of occupation did the Egyptian army build and maintain substantial fortifications. From these secure bases, the Egyptian soldiers could strike out at enemy forces, patrol trade routes, and collect taxes and tribute from vassal states. While natural features, such as the First Cataract of the Nile, the Sinai Desert, and the Mediterranean coast, provided Egypt with its traditional borders, a number of strong, military pharaohs declared their intention to extend the borders of the kingdom. Tuthmosis I (1,504–1,492 BC) of the Eighteenth Dynasty proved most successful and he was able to conquer both Palestine and Syria all the way to the banks of the Euphrates River. In the south, his territory was marked by the Kurgus boundary stele (located between the Fourth and Fifth Cataracts in Upper Nubia). Yet his gains were fleeting; the northern frontier in the centuries that followed usually lay somewhere in southern Syria, while the southern frontier sat at the Second Cataract in Lower Nubia, guarded by the fortress at Buhen.

Egyptians had settled around the Second Cataract region as long ago as the Old Kingdom, in order to exploit Lower Nubia's many animal and mineral resources. However, it was during the Middle Kingdom that significant militarisation of the area occurred, effectively moving the southern frontier of Egypt from the First Cataract at Aswan south to the Second Cataract. A string of heavily defended forts, interspersed with look-out stations, was constructed along the Nile to the north and south of the Second Cataract. The papyrus called *Ramesseum Onomasticon* records some of the belligerent titles used to name these forts and they included the 'Warding off the Bows', 'Repelling the Seti', and 'Curbing the Countries'.

Buhen, a magnificent mud-brick fort, located at the northern end of the Second Cataract region, served as the command centre for the military build-up of the Middle Kingdom. The forts it controlled were established in order to control the acquisition and transportation of trade goods to Egypt; they provided a base for campaigns southwards into Upper Nubia and served also to protect the border of Egypt. During the New Kingdom, with Lower Nubia virtually pacified, the defensive purpose of the forts declined and a large amount

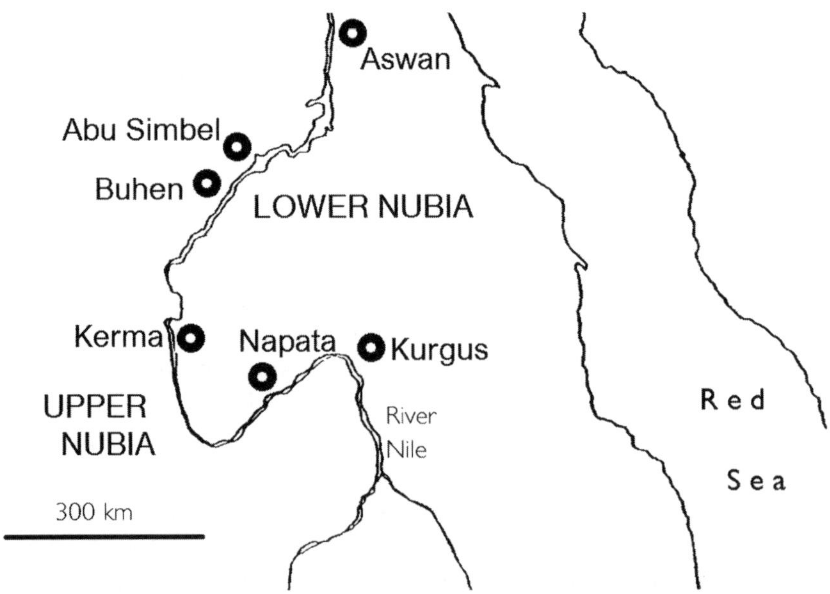

of civilian settlement occurred around and between them. Buhen, like several of the other forts, was a rectangular structure, yet this super-fort boasted an outer enclosure wall over 700 metres long and 4 metres thick. At regular intervals, the wall was strengthened by thirty-two semi-circular bastions and its western wall featured several much larger towers and an impressive central gateway—known today as the Barbican. In the New Kingdom, this gate tower measured 47 × 30 metres and was defended by a drawbridge, a double sets of doors, and two baffle entrances. An inner wall with its own towers and bastions stood 11 metres high and added yet another layer of protection. Other defensive features, such as archery loopholes, glacis, and berms, were also present at Buhen.

Most of the forts of the Second Cataract had similar grid-like plans, with well-laid out streets, barracks, storerooms, and officers' quarters; some even had access to the Nile via a walled or covered stairway. At the fortress called Iken (modern Mirgissa), archaeologists discovered a cache of spears and arrows and a number of shields that were in various stages of construction. Where geography restricted the designs of architects and engineers, they had to adapt the plan of the fort to suit the terrain. Look-out posts consisted of roughly built stone houses that were located at strategic points on the cliffs above the Nile. We know that look-outs at Semna fort recorded all the comings and goings of the local people. Their intelligence reports were passed back to central command at Thebes:

> ...the soldier Nekhen came to report ... on a mission from the officer of the town regiment ... Khusobek ... who is acting in lieu of the officer of the sovereign's crew in the garrison of Meha, saying: 'The patrol that went out to patrol the desert edge near the fortress of Khesef-Medjau on the last day of the third month of spring in the third year has returned to report to me, saying: "We have found the track of 32 men and 3 donkeys ..."'
>
> Semna Dispatches

To counter increased threats from the Near Eastern powers during the New Kingdom, fortresses and garrison towns were built to defend the borders of the Nile Delta. The Ramesside fortifications of Tell el-Heir in the eastern Delta and Zawiyet Umm el-Rakham, 340 km to the west of Alexandria, were a part of this military build-up. Ramses II also built a string of forts out into Libyan territory that terminated at Umm el-Rakham. Piramesse was a new city probably founded by Ramses I that served as a major military centre during the Nineteenth Dynasty. Its location in the eastern Delta reflected a growing threat from the Hittite Empire, which was based northwards in Turkey and had ambitions in Syria that were to inevitably clash with those of Egypt. Piramesse was too far from the fighting to serve as a frontier defence; instead, the city became a military depot and jumping off point for military campaigns into Palestine and Syria. Manfred Bietak, leading a team of Austrian archaeologists in an excavation at the site, discovered evidence of a well-organised system of stabling for chariot horses.

By the time of Amenhotep III (1,391–1,353 BC), Egypt had established several military garrisons in Palestine, although these did not form a true occupation force. Egyptian strategy in the Near East allowed the city-states a large measure of independence, they were vassal kingdoms, owing fealty to the pharaoh and sending regular shipments of tribute to him. Garrison troops were there to ensure the safety of Egyptian scribes, officials, and diplomats and to see that the tributes were duly despatched. It was also important to prevent the interference of a rival state or empire from meddling with Palestinian politics. Garrisons are known to have been established at the cities of Sharuhen, Irqata, Megiddo, Gezer, Byblos, Sumera, and Ullaza, as well as a number of lesser sites. Likewise, administrative bases were set up at the coastal centres of Joppa and Gaza.

It seems that these garrisons were composed mainly of native Egyptian infantrymen or Nubian archers, usually with a supporting arm of chariotry. Few soldiers were needed for this role—both Megiddo and Gezer only required a garrison of 100 men each, while many other cities were kept under control with as few as fifty. Requests were occasionally made to pharaoh for additional troops to aid a city's battle against bandits or, more often, against the forces of a neighbouring city-state. In a similar vein, both the post-2005 Iraqi government and the Afghan National Army made repeated requests to the US and UK governments for more 'boots on the ground' in their own battles against local insurgent forces. The Egyptians will no doubt have been cynical about some of these requests for military assistance, and they were reluctant to become embroiled in long-standing grudges between city-states.

4

The Nine Bows

Take to thyself the sword, O mighty king, whose mace smites the Nine Bows.

Inscription of Seti I on the walls of the temple of Amun at Karnak

Due to the importance of the bow in military and political iconography, Egypt referred to its nine traditional enemies as the Nine Bows. The identity of these historical tribes and kingdoms varied from century to century, but the theme of the Nine Bows was repeated endlessly on royal inscriptions. Occasionally, the artists would depict a row of actual bows, at other times, the Nine Bows would appear as bound captives being led before the king. The official seal of the Valley of the Kings necropolis depicted nine bound captives that were surmounted by a jackal. These particular Nine Bows intended to protect the mummified bodies of the pharaohs from the evils of foreign intervention.

The enemies of Egypt varied in their social development, military sophistication, and general level of threat. This required Egypt to tailor its military response to an invasion or attack based on the nature of the aggressor. Pharaohs of the Old Kingdom had created suitable strategies to deal with the Nubian and Libyan tribes that formed the traditional foes of Egypt. Threats from the Near East, however, proved more problematic—as the Hyksos takeover had illustrated. The region most hotly contested is often referred to today as the 'Fertile Crescent' since it stretches northwards in an arc of agricultural land from Sinai in the south through Palestine and Syria, to the mountains of eastern Turkey in the north; it then curves eastwards and then south to encompass the fertile river valleys of the Euphrates and Tigris. The continents of Africa and Asia met within this region, and the powers, states, cities, and tribes that existed there, met, traded, and waged war. While long-lived dynasties of pharaohs ruled a stable and peaceful Egypt for century after century, the situation within the Near East was always volatile, always politically unstable, and subject to invasion and tribal migration. Kingdoms, empires, and states rose and fell, with

none able to seize and then hold the city-states of Syria and Palestine (an area known by the French term 'Levant') for more than a century or two. With the expulsion of the Hyksos rulers in 1,540 BC and Ahmose I's military campaign into Palestine soon after, Egypt had stepped into this tumultuous arena for the first time. However, was the newly reformed military machine of Egypt any match for the belligerent empires and powerful city-states that vied for control of the Fertile Crescent?

Pharaoh Ahmose (1,550–1,525 BC) had left Egypt united, powerful, and economically stable, and there is little doubt that the kingdom had become the chief power in the Near East at that time. Ahmose's son, Amenhotep I (1,525–1,504 BC), left few details of his exploits—although we do know that he despatched the army south into Kush. At his death, we get a glimpse of the power that the army now held in both society and in government. For Amenhotep I was not succeeded by his son, but instead (and breaking with an age old tradition) by a middle-aged and experienced general named Tuthmosis I (1,504–1,492 BC). Although his reign lasted only a decade, it was marked by aggressive military campaigns into Syria that took the Egyptian armies to the very banks of the Euphrates River, further than they had ever travelled before. In the south, he conquered the Nubian tribes and pushed Egyptian sovereignty as far as Kurgus, midway between the Fourth and Fifth Cataracts. A soldier who embarked on these campaigns payed tribute to his pharaoh:

> He brought the ends of the earth into his domain. He reached as far as its extremities with his mighty sword, seeking battle, but he found no-one who could face him. He penetrated the lands that were unknown to his royal ancestors.... His southern boundary is as far as the frontier of this land, (his) northern as far as that inverted water which goes down-stream in going up-stream.
>
> Tombos Stela, written by an unknown officer in Tuthmosis I's army

The strange remarks about a river which 'goes down-stream in going up-stream' refers to the Euphrates, and it illustrates the parochial mind-set of the Egyptians at that point. In Egypt, rivers (as the Nile shows) should flow from south to north. Here, the Euphrates, equal in size and importance to the Nile, was not obeying that natural order.

Critics of George W. Bush's invasion of Iraq in 2003 claimed that his administration was motivated by revenge for the 9/11 attacks and a desire to strike strategically at states that might (at some point in the future) pose a threat to the US. We can see Tuthmosis' long-range campaigns in the same vein—an attack on neighbouring states designed not just to punish, but to pre-empt any future enemy invasion. Power and security were now key to Egyptian strategy, no longer could the inhabitants of the Nile valley content themselves with peace and happiness at home.

Little attempt was made to consolidate these military forays into an empire, however. Such an undertaking had to wait until the grandson of Tuthmosis I took power and began building a true Egyptian empire. Tuthmosis I died around 1,492 BC, his eldest sons tragically dying before him. The third young son became pharaoh and was married off to the eldest daughter of Tuthmosis I, the girl Hatshepsut, in order to strengthen his position. The pair ruled for fourteen years until Tuthmosis II died while in his early thirties. His son, Tuthmosis III (1,479–1,425 BC), was obviously too young to rule and so his step-mother, Hatshepsut (1,473–1,458 BC), acted first as regent and then as the queen of Egypt in her own right. Baby Menkheperre, who would be declared the pharaoh's successor, and who took the name Tuthmosis III, was not the union of Hatshepsut and the king—pharaohs had many wives and consorts, and Menkheperre or Tuthmosis III was borne by Isis, a girl within the king's harem.

Within two years of Hatshepsut's death, Tuthmosis III had launched an aggressive military campaign into Syria; Egyptologists have since nicknamed him 'the Napoleon of Ancient Egypt'.

Amorite City-States

The Amorites were a group of Semitic tribes that spread into the Fertile Crescent around 2,000 BC, where they established towns, cities, and dynasties, including the kingdom of the Hyksos that comprised both Canaan and the Egyptian Delta. The land of Canaan encompassed a narrow region laying between the Mediterranean Sea and the River Jordan (as well as the Dead Sea into which it flowed). This strip of fertile land was the 'Land of Milk and Honey' that would later be settled by the Hebrews around 1,100 BC. Its most powerful cities were Joppa, Sharuhen, Megiddo, Shechem, Lachish, Jerusalem, and Hazor. The Egyptians called this land Djahy, but we know it today as Palestine.

A narrow coastal plain rises inland to a line of mountains that then falls away steeply into the Jordan valley. Further east, a second line of mountains separates the Jordan from the dry steppes and deserts of northern Arabia. Two main trade routes passed through Palestine: the first, the King's Highway, followed the edge of the steppe-lands to the east of the Jordan valley, while the 'Way of the Sea' ran along the coastal plain and through the cities of Raphia, Gaza, and Joppa. Its way north to Megiddo and Acco was blocked by Mount Carmel, which ran out westwards to form a headland on the coast. Travellers (or armies) were forced to negotiate difficult mountain passes if they wished to reach the broad Syrian plains to the north.

Egypt knew Syria as Amurru, the Land of the Amorites. To reach it, the traveller passed Mount Carmel, and on through Lebanon, two more north-south mountain ranges that were separated by the Bekaa valley. A large inland plain, watered by the River Orontes, dominated Syria, which was cultivated by farmers of the great city-states—places like Hamath, Kadesh, Aleppo, Carchemish, Haran, and Qatna. The powerful seaports of Byblos, Ugarit, Tyre, and Sidon hugged the Syrian coast. Generally of great age, the cities had been rebuilt many times over many centuries, raising them up on to artificially created hills, or 'tells'. Unlike the cities of Egypt, those in the Near East were nearly all fortified, with high encircling walls, towers, and gateways—enemies existed all around.

None of the cities formed any meaningful political unions, although some of the more powerful states were able to assemble *ad hoc* and short-lived alliances. Inter-state warfare was endemic, and Amorite nomads—such as the Shaasu and Sutu Bedouin and a wandering tribe of mercenaries and nomads called the Habiru—regularly attacked the settled lands. Some think that these Habiru might well be the Hebrews. In a Cold War-style stand-off, the Egyptian, Mitanni, and Hittite kings all exploited the local Syrian and Canaanite rivalries to their own advantage. For their own part, some of the local kings attempted to play the imperial powers off against one another.

Despite their small size and petty politics, the city-states were able to field quite sophisticated and effective military forces. The Hyksos, it should be remembered, were Amorite kings who brought their military technology with them to Egypt. The perpetual warfare and rivalry between the city-states probably contributed to the hot-house development of military thinking. Like the Hyksos, the armies of Canaan and Syria relied on a core of elite chariotry

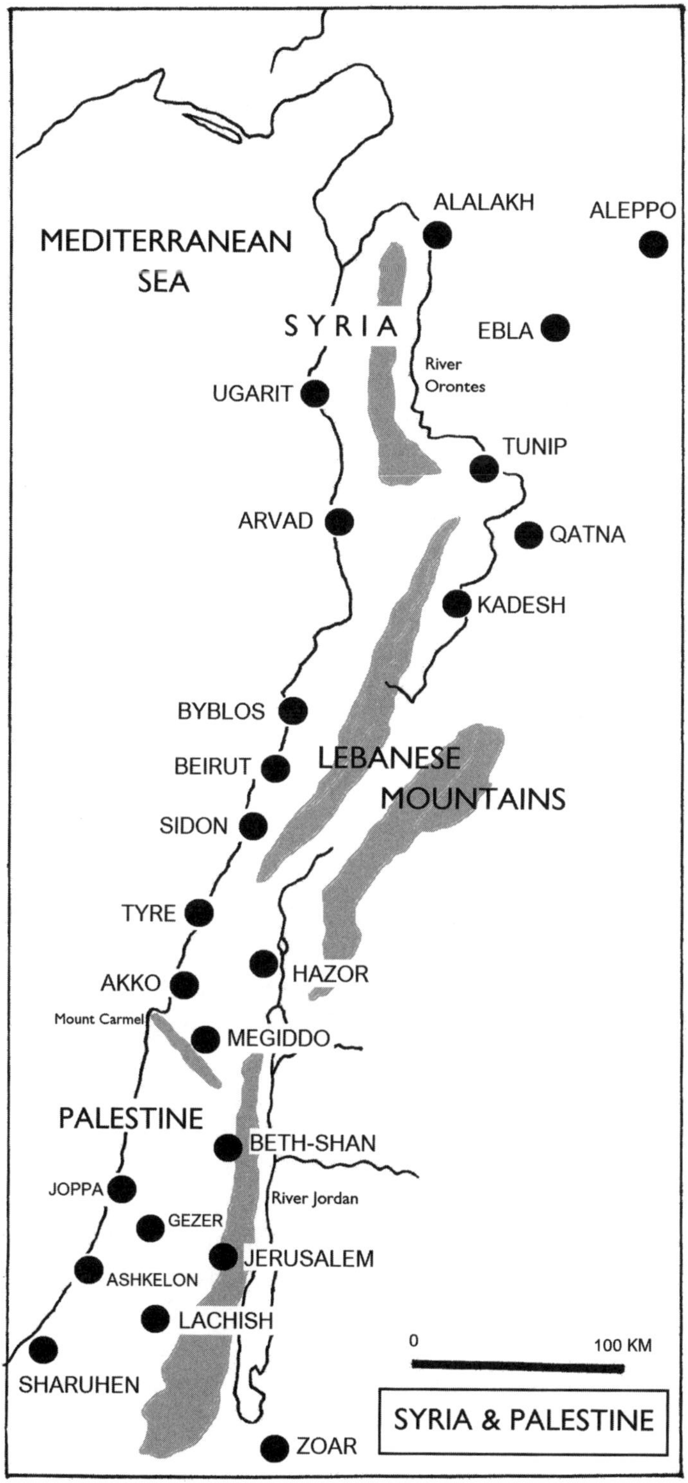

SYRIA & PALESTINE

known as *maryannu*. Another term, *ne'arin*, occurs in some Egyptian texts as a reference to Canaanite enemies; it is also used in Hebrew texts as a word to describe elite troops. The term may have originated within the powerful Syrian city-state of Ugarit, where it is used to describe hereditary chariot-warriors.

These men were the nobility of Canaan and Syria; they entered battle wearing bronze scale armour, shared their two-horse chariot with a driver, and were supported by a 'runner' or foot soldier and a number of grooms. The *maryannu* concept had been developed originally by the Mitanni, but this 'tactical package' was adopted wholesale by all of the states of the Fertile Crescent. In a manner similar to Medieval feudalism, the kings awarded the status of *maryannu* to members of the landed nobility, although wealthy merchants and high-status craftsmen may also have served, providing their own arms, armour, and chariot-team.

Like the Hyksos, the chariot troops formed a shock missile unit that proved devastating to infantry and could only be successfully countered by rival chariotry. The king of a city would ride in his own chariot and be accompanied into battle by an elite retinue of *maryannu*. Much of the rest of the army was comprised of either peasant conscripts (*hupshu*), foreign mercenaries (mainly desert Bedouin), and, in some cases, garrison troops provided by one of the imperial powers. Infantry were unarmoured and fought either as spearmen or archers, but they were inferior to their Egyptian counterparts, serving only as a supporting arm to their *maryannu* masters.

The Battle of Megiddo

As a young prince, Tuthmosis III seems to have been shunted off to the army, allowing his half-sister a free reign to rule the kingdom. Within two years of taking the throne, the (now) experienced military youth led the Egyptian army north on a campaign of domination and subjugation against the city states of Canaan. Egyptologists are incredibly lucky to be able to study records kept by the chief military scribe who accompanied the expedition, a man named Thaneni. The Annals of Tuthmosis III that he penned form the most complete account of the military achievements of any Egyptian king, yet it is plain that the campaigns of other pharaohs were also recorded, just like the Annals, on rolls of parchment that were then archived at the temple of Amun at Karnak.

Had Hatshepsut herself campaigned northwards into Canaan with the Egyptian army, then Tuthmosis I's gains might have been secured. As it was, his victories were quickly lost. Tuthmosis III was forced to act when it became clear that the Syrian city of Megiddo, on the banks of the Orontes River, was fomenting a great northern revolt. In 1,456 BC, all of Egypt's enemies were gathering together to build an army with which to challenge the suzerainty of Egypt north of Canaan, it included many of the Amorite city-states and had the backing of the Mitanni empire. This powerful empire ruled all of the lands at the headwaters of the Euphrates and Tigris rivers, and its king at this time (most probably King Parrattarna) had every reason to oppose an Egyptian frontier that ended right at his door-step, on the bank of the Euphrates river.

In Tuthmosis' second year as sole ruler (his twenty-third as co-ruler with Hatshepsut), he led a mighty army northwards to deal with upstart Megiddo and stamp Egyptian authority onto the region. His army travelled quickly across the Sinai desert, drawing water from wells that had been dug along the desert roads. After reaching Gaza, the speed of the column dropped from 24 km to about 12 km per day, either due to fatigue or security—the army was now in potentially hostile territory. General Djehuty was detached with a force large enough and capable enough to successfully besiege the city of Jaffa. Tuthmosis III considered the city a threat that offered a danger to his expedition.

When the Egyptian expedition reached the Plain of Sharon, the commanders of the army found themselves faced with a number of difficult choices. Mountains lay between them and Megiddo. Would they take the army along an easy route, where any ambush could be easily countered, or should they take the pass of Aruna? This was a narrow defile that would leave the army no room to manoeuvre should an ambush by the forces of Megiddo be sprung. After deliberation with his senior staff officers in a council of war, Tuthmosis III decided to risk the outcome of the war, his life, and his reputation on the dangerous path of Aruna. It was the quicker route and would allow the army to deploy less than 2 km from the city gates. However, if the enemy had the heights above it occupied, the pass would prove a death-trap, and for that very reason, pharaoh's generals had all counselled against using it.

Perhaps the vehemence with which his own council of war argued against the Aruna path convinced Tuthmosis that the Canaanite commanders might actually be thinking the very same thing—that they might be utterly discounting it as a potential invasion route. The alternative, particularly the one via Taanach, was a much easier march onto the Plain of Esdraelon but one that would almost certainly be defended by enemy forces. Before Tuthmosis could even deploy his army for battle, it would have faced a withering onslaught from massed chariot attacks and a rain of arrows from Canaanite archers. The Egyptian commanders thought this option held better odds than the difficult mountain pass.

Two days of marching brought the army into the pass, at its widest only 10 metres across, and it is a measure of the Egyptian army's size that it took twelve hours for all of the troops and their baggage to pass safely through. Tuthmosis' gamble had paid off and as the army safely deployed onto the Plain of Esdraelon, the Canaanite forces had to rapidly redeploy outside the city of Megiddo.

> Then was set up the camp of his majesty and command was given to the whole army, saying 'Equip yourselves! Prepare your weapons! For we shall advance

> to fight with that wretched foe in the morning'.... The watch of the army went about saying, 'Steady of heart! Steady of heart! Be watchful! Be watchful!'
>
> The Annals

Clearly the Egyptians feared a night attack, and although the pharaoh is made to sound confident and ebullient, we can be sure that his soldiers did not. Should the battle tomorrow go against them, the Egyptians were faced with a long march back to safety across rugged mountain terrain. Cities behind them would not be so welcoming on their return, and seeing the Egyptian army in defeat, were extremely likely to switch their allegiance and fall in with the northern coalition of states.

The chief scribe Thaneni related that, in the morning, the pharaoh led his army from a chariot of electrum out onto the plain before the fortified city of Megiddo. Tuthmosis III, like all pharaohs before him, will have worn the blue crown, a crown worn only in wartime. 'Command was given for the entire army to move' and its deployment is described clearly in the Annals. The northern wing of the army was deployed to the north-west of Megiddo, the southern wing occupied a low hill to the south of the 'brook of' Kina. Pharaoh, his guard chariot squadron, his officers, and attendants occupied the centre, between the wings of the army. Meanwhile, the king of Megiddo and the chiefs that he had rallied to his cause were deploying their own troops outside the city.

Little is known of the numbers involved in the battle of Megiddo and neither are there any records of how the battle progressed. All that is known for certain is that 'his majesty prevailed against them at the head of his army, and when they saw (this) they fled headlong to Megiddo'.

The victory must have been swift, and this implies a charge of chariots, no doubt led by Tuthmosis III himself, since the enemy lines collapsed and the Canaanites routed. Chariots, weapons, and military standards of the Canaanites littered the battlefield, abandoned by the panicked soldiers, and 'their champions lay stretched out like fishes on the ground'. Defenders within Megiddo, terrified that Tuthmosis would enter the city and annihilate its population, closed the gates, trapping most of the Canaanite army outside the walls. Desperately calling up to the battlements, many of the frightened troops (the kings of Megiddo and Kadesh among them) were hastily hauled up into the city by ropes or knotted sheets. Megiddo was, for now, safe from the wrath of the Egyptians.

The Annals blame the failure of the Egyptian army to capture the city on the greed of the troops. By stopping to plunder the bodies and the baggage of the Canaanite forces, they had given the enemy enough time to reach the city and for the city gates to be closed. However, a good deal of booty was captured, including expensive war chariots, gold, silver, prisoners of war, horses, and, of course, piles of blood smeared and sand encrusted human hands.

Now the city had to be besieged, 'for every chief of every country that has revolted, is within it, and its capture is the capture of a thousand cities'. Egyptian troops dug a ditch around Megiddo and constructed a wooden palisade. Pharaoh and his men settled in for a long siege, and in December 1,456 BC, seven months later, the city surrendered, rendering up a huge amount of booty to the Egyptian crown. Following an account of the surrender of Megiddo, the Annals proceed to list the spoils captured by pharaoh, although much on the list sounds like battlefield plunder. There are tent poles covered with silver, a couple of chariots of the chiefs decorated with gold, 892 other chariots, more than 200 suits of bronze scale armour, 502 bows, six stallions, 191 foals, and 2,041 mares. Much of this war booty is unlikely to have made it into Megiddo after the battle, keeping in mind that the gates were shut on the fleeing troops. The recovered equipment thus provides us with some idea of the size of the Canaanite force involved. Included in the scribe's tally are more than 20,000 cattle, no doubt presented to the Egyptians by the people of Megiddo as tribute.

With Megiddo at last defeated and the lords of Canaan forced to pay homage to the pharaoh, Tuthmosis III had brought southern Syria to heel in a single decisive battle. Once he had taken three more cities—Yenoam, Nuges, and Herenkeru—that all owed fealty to the king of Kadesh, Tuthmosis III returned in triumph to Thebes. For the next eighteen years, Tuthmosis led annual military campaigns into southern Syria in an attempt to wrestle control of this region away from the king of Kadesh and his overlord, the great king of Mitanni. At last, in year forty-two of his reign, the pharaoh was able to capture Kadesh and yet it proved to be only one in a roll call of defeated cities that numbered more than 350. Accounts of these expeditions make it clear that the Egyptian navy was being routinely used to ship troops to and from the Syrian area of operations. It is with some justification that John Henry Breasted called Tuthmosis III the 'Napoleon of ancient Egypt'.

Nubians

The land of Nubia is today split between Egypt and Sudan and its people are of black African descent. Nubia stretched from Aswan southwards, running along the fertile banks of the Nile as far as modern Khartoum. Away from the lush river banks, nomads herded goats and cattle on the dry grasslands that skirted the edge of the desert. The northernmost part of Nubia, from Aswan to Wadi Halfa, was known as Lower Nubia, but the region was flooded during the construction and filling of the Aswan High Dam in the 1960s (modern Egyptians refer to the High Dam as the 'Russian Dam' as opposed to the 'British Dam' that was built in 1902). During the New Kingdom, Lower Nubia was conquered and then governed directly by Egypt. It became known as *Ta-sety* ('Land of the Bow') or as Kush. Pharaoh Tuthmosis III launched campaigns on the territory of Upper Nubia, further south, and was able to successfully capture the Nubian capital of Kerma, which pushed the border of Egypt southwards to the Fourth Cataract. Nubia was pacified, although its warriors continued to find employment within the Egyptian army.

This new region was governed by a 'Viceroy of Kush', a man appointed personally by the pharaoh to rule this southerly land in his name. Among the viceroy's many tasks were building projects, military affairs, administration and the exploitation and collection of all the valuable resources (in particular gold and good quality building stone) that Nubia had to offer. So much gold did Nubia produce that one of the viceroy's secondary titles was 'Overseer of the Gold Lands of the Lord of Two Lands'. He was assisted by two deputies who themselves ruled subdivisions of the province, Wawat (Lower Nubia) and Kush (Upper Nubia). This arrangement differed from the Egyptian extension of power into Syria and Palestine, where Canaanite kings were able to freely rule their city-states on behalf of pharaoh. Again, contrary to policy in Syria and Palestine, a programme of 'Egyptianisation' was carried out in Nubia, encouraging the local people to adopt Egyptian manners and customs, dress, and language. Sons of Nubian chiefs were routinely taken hostage and educated downriver at Thebes, in Egyptian ways. Later, they were sent back to their homeland to rule their local chiefdoms with an Egyptian perspective. Several of these Nubian chiefs established recognisably Egyptian dynasties that helped to promote the values of the northern superpower. In many parts of Lower Nubia, the indigenous C-Group Nubian culture was completely replaced during the New Kingdom by one that began to construct Egyptian houses and tombs, and which enjoyed all of the material benefits of Egyptian goods.

During the Eighteenth Dynasty, the large forts clustered around the Second Cataract, which had defended Egypt from the Nubians during the Middle and early New Kingdom, were transformed from military garrisons into centres of administration, trade, and mining. Towns and temples were also constructed there to both facilitate trade and spread Egyptian culture throughout the region. During the reign of the Nineteenth Dynasty Pharaoh Ramses II, two of the greatest temples in ancient Egypt were constructed at Abu Simbel, in Lower Nubia. Although they formed part of a grand series, strung along the upper Nile, the two rock-cut tombs of Abu Simbel were the most immense and most impressive pieces of Ramses' imperial propaganda. The lessons of humility and subservience were hammered home by Ramses who employed prisoners of war that had been captured by the pharaoh's campaigns in Nubia to build the two great temples.

Nubian society was traditionally organised around the tribe and the Egyptians record the Medjay, Wawat, Setju, and Irtjet tribes, among others. It is clear that by the start of the New Kingdom, these tribes were united by a royal dynasty based at Kerma on the border of Upper and Lower Nubia. Nubian war bands did not possess the chariot which meant that all of its warriors were foot soldiers. Without access to the training and the discipline of the Egyptian forces, the Nubian warriors were forced to fight in the only way they knew how, in loose formations, attacking their enemies in small skirmish units or in waves of massed soldiers. Nubians were skilled bowmen throughout their history and were valued by the pharaohs as mercenary troops. The models within the tomb of Mesehti at Asyut and the cache of mummified soldiers that were discovered by Herbert Winlock attest to this fact.

Nubians fought in clothes of leather or animal hide and many reliefs show their warriors clad in cheetah, antelope, or lion skins (complete with tail). Jewellery, in the form of earrings, armlets, necklaces, and bracelets, were also commonly worn into battle (and must have been sought after as booty by victorious Egyptian troops), while ostrich feathers or headbands adorned the head. Nubian tribes had little access to metal, which meant that their weapons typically consisted of clubs, javelins, and daggers, but the main weapon of the country was always the stave bow. Arrows were carried in the hand or tucked into a waist sash, along with a dagger. Nubian shields were oval in shape and probably of a wicker construction that was faced with animal hide.

Libyans

The huge area west of the Nile, as far north as the Mediterranean and as far south as Nubia, was called Libya in antiquity. The tribes inhabiting this vast wilderness of rock waste, sandy desert, and dry grassland made repeated inroads into the Nile valley over the centuries. Two large Libyan tribes were known to the Egyptians, the Tehennu and the Temehu, and they survived by herding cattle and goats and from the game that they could hunt on the trail. Periods of hardship and drought eventually drove these nomads into the western Delta where they clashed with the local Egyptian authorities. At the end of the New Kingdom, new tribes emerged from the Libyan steppe (including the Shai, the Meshwesh, the Kehek, and the Libu), driven eastwards by the slow but relentless desiccation of the eastern Sahara.

The western oases, which sat remote from the safety of the Nile valley, served as outposts against Libyan migration. High-quality dates and grapes were grown at these oases, but they also served as trade links to more remote areas. The four great oases were, from north to south, Bahariya, Farafra, el-Dakhla, and el-Kharga. So remote were these islands of civilisation that fugitives from Egyptian justice sometimes fled to them in search of safety and anonymity. During the Twenty-First Dynasty, the oases of el-Dakhla and el-Kharga also served as penal colonies, a place out in the Libyan wilderness to which political undesirables could be exiled.

Traditionally, the Libyan tribes fought with javelins, throw-sticks, and stave bows. Their tactics resembled those of the Nubians, skirmishing from a distance, striking from ambush, or rushing in waves upon their Egyptian foes. Like most tribal armies, the Libyans fought in loose formations, organised most likely by bloodline or tribal allegiance rather than tactical necessity. In one instance, Libyan warriors mounted a surprise attack at dawn, presumably using the poor light to their own advantage. Faced with Egyptian organisation, discipline, and weapons technology, Libyan success in war had to focus on ambush tactics and the hit-and-run raid.

During the reign of Nineteenth Dynasty pharaohs Merenptah and Ramses III, both Libyan tactics and Libyan military organisation took a dramatic turn. A coalition of displaced peoples, refugees, mercenaries, and nomads descended on Egypt *en masse*. These 'Sea Peoples' are dealt with in more detail in the next chapter, but it is important to understand that the Libyans threw their lot in with the Sea Peoples. A newly appointed commander-in-chief led a vast host of newly emerged Libyan tribes into the Delta to face the beleaguered Egyptian army. The scale of these attacks dwarfed earlier Libyan raids, and in defeat, many of the warriors were settled within military cantonments to form a hereditary caste of ethnic Libyan warriors, fighting in later wars as the '*Meshwesh*'. These later Libyan warriors, working in close co-operation with the Sea Peoples, had access to small numbers of chariots and to large quantities of spears and longswords.

The physical appearance of Libyan tribesmen on the Egyptian reliefs is quite striking, they often appear almost naked with only a fabric sheath or sash covering the groin; this sheath or sash seems to be attached to a waist belt. Some warriors are also shown wearing a heavy cloak of animal hide that might have been used as a defensive item, since Libyan fighters are never shown with shields. As in Egypt, ostrich feathers held some kind of special significance and are worn by some of the Libyan tribesmen and their chiefs in the Egyptian reliefs. The hair of these men is braided, and their bodies are often decorated (either with tattoos or war paint—the reliefs are very unclear). Some of the warriors are shown with bands crossing the chest, probably made up of beadwork, which may have served as some kind of body armour.

5

New Enemies

As for the foreign countries, they made a conspiracy in their sea-lands.... A camp [was set up] in one place in Amor. They desolated its people and its land was like that which has never come into being. They were coming, while the flame was prepared before them, forward into Egypt.

Inscription of Ramses III at Medinet Habu, describing an attack on the Delta by the Sea Peoples.

The petty kings and princelings of Palestine and Syria often proved a thorn in Egypt's side, but recalcitrant rulers could usually be brought to heel by a punitive Egyptian expedition. For the pharaohs of the Eighteenth Dynasty, the real enemy lay further north, among the upper reaches of the Tigris and Euphrates rivers. Here, in northern Syria, an empire known to the Egyptians as Naharin or Mitanni was established some time after 1,600 BC. The different names seem to have referred to the same kingdom and were used interchangeably according to Michael Astour.

Kingdom of Mitanni

Mitanni grew from the amalgamation of various small mountain states populated by a people called the Hurrians, although the power behind Mitanni actually lay with a foreign Indo-Aryan aristocracy that had earlier migrated down from the Iranian plateau. These warlike, chariot-owning noblemen were called the *maryannu* and they were a social elite that easily dominated the local Hurrian tribes and welded them into a powerful and aggressive military force. Aryan chariot tactics, coupled with the Hurrian expertise in manufacturing coats of lamellar and scale armour, allowed the Mitanni to reign supreme on the battlefield. Mitanni influence was widespread, initiating a military revolution across the Near East. Not only Egyptian, but Canaanite, Assyrian, Elamite, and Kassite armies all adopted the Mitanni way of war.

Washukanni, the capital city of the Mitanni empire, has not been satisfactorily identified in the archaeological record. It is often suggested that the city of the Mitanni was at Tell el-Fakhariyeh, west of Tell Brak on the bank of the Habur river; however, some academics have argued against this location.

Mitanni could not have emerged as a regional power within the shadow of the great empires of the day—in particular, the kingdom of Old Babylon, established by Hammurabi in 1,792 BC. Hammurabi's Babylonia stretched from one end of Mesopotamia to the other and its armies were strong, well-equipped, and well-trained. Yet this powerful empire, which had successfully dominated the Euphrates and Tigris valleys for two centuries, was suddenly brought to an end when Babylon was sacked by an invading army in 1,595 BC. A distant people located in central Anatolia, known today as the Hittites, had emerged onto the world stage and did so with a devastating blow that brought down Babylon with fire and violence. Mesopotamia quickly entered a dark age that lasted some 150 years, about which historians and archaeologists know virtually nothing.

It is within this power vacuum that the state of Mitanni developed, for the Hittites retreated to Anatolia after sacking Babylon and would not return to Syria for some time. The Mitanni empire that was ruled from Washukanni encompassed parts of Mesopotamia to the east (probably demanding tribute from the tiny kingdom of Assyria), the Hurri-lands of the mountains, and the

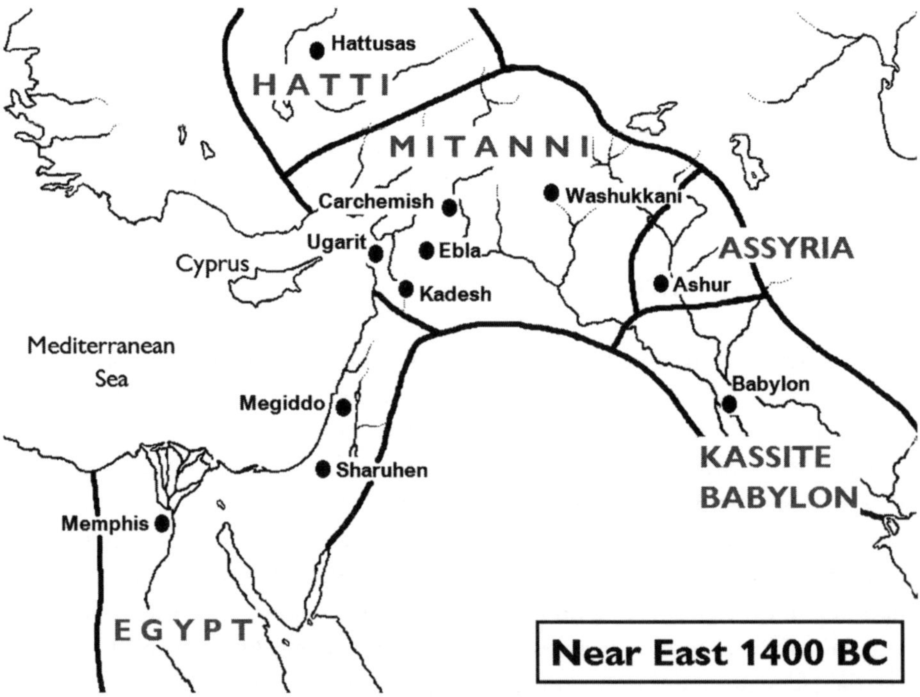

wealthy caravan cities of northern Syria, such as Carchemish, Harran, Aleppo, Emar, Qatna, and Kadesh. Throughout the fifteenth century BC, the vigorous kings Parrattarna and Saushtatar pushed the rule of Mitanni ever southwards. Tuthmosis III stood against this Mitanni expansion, taking first Megiddo and then Kadesh and its neighbouring cities. This aggressive pharaoh expanded the territory of New Kingdom Egypt at the expense of the Mitanni empire.

The Battle of Naharin

Tuthmosis' relentless assaults on the Syrian cities paved the way for an all-out confrontation with the Mitanni empire. In year thirty-three (1,445 BC) of his reign, pharaoh led the army northwards once again and it was reinforced at several stages along the route by additional Egyptian troops disembarking from ships at ports along the coast. After crossing the River Orontes, the large Egyptian force had its first encounter with the Mitanni outside the city of Aleppo. The Annals mention only one decisive battle, although one officer of the Egyptian army, Amenemhab, fortunately related his military career on the walls of his own tomb. Amenemhab speaks of three separate battles in Naharin (the land of Mitanni); in particular, he named a clash of armies to the west of Aleppo and a final, more decisive battle at Carchemish, on the Euphrates River. Here, the army crossed the river on a pontoon bridge using timber it had previously cut from the Lebanese forests. Tuthmosis took his army south along the left bank of the river, but failed to bring the Mitanni king to battle. The pharaoh had to satisfy himself with the erection of a commemorative victory stela next to one that had been set up by his grandfather, Tuthmosis I, during his foray west of the Euphrates.

Washukanni, the Mitanni capital, would never fall to the Egyptian army and neither the 'Napoleon of ancient Egypt' nor his successors would ever meet the Mitanni king in battle. Tuthmosis III valiantly fought to keep the enemy out of Syria until he was too old to venture forth in person and his generals instead continued the struggle. Yet the effort and expense involved in maintaining a grip on distant Syria could not easily be maintained. By the time of Tuthmosis' death, it is clear that Mitanni was once again meddling in Syrian affairs.

Amenhotep II (1,427–1,401 BC), the son of Tuthmosis III, had to refight many of his father's battles, since most of the Palestinian and Syrian city-states revolted at hearing of the old pharaoh's death. It seems that treaty agreements with these cities were made with an individual Egyptian king and not the state itself. This loss of control meant that Mitanni was able to renew its foothold within the region, until the time came when both empires were forced to reach a rapprochement. A new threat had emerged, or re-emerged—the Hittites from central Anatolia, who had so successfully smashed the power of Babylon in 1,595

BC, were now attempting to establish their own presence in Syria, and this put Mitanni directly in the firing line. Egypt, too, stood to lose all of its gains in the region, and so by the reigns of Tuthmosis IV (1,401–1,391 BC) and Amenhotep III (1,391–1,351 BC), the two great powers were working together and alliances were sealed through the long-standing practice of diplomatic marriage. Some of these diplomatic *communiqués* are recorded on the Amarna tablets, found within the abandoned Egyptian city of Amarna (that was later to be constructed by Amenhotep III's son, Akhenaten). These tablets provide Egyptologists with wonderful details about Egypt's relationship with the squabbling princes and kings of Palestine and Syria. With their inward-looking inter-city rivalries and their ongoing problems with desert migrants like the Sutu and the Habiru, the city-states could never hope to be free of outside interference from the great powers of the day.

Kingdom of Hatti

Throughout the Bronze Age, Anatolia, the rugged and mountainous land that is known today as Turkey, was home to an enigmatic people known as the Hittites. For several centuries, the princes and kings of the 'Land of Hatti' remained in their mountain fastness until King Mursilis I (1,620–1,590 BC) led the armies of Hatti into northern Syria in a bloody campaign that ended with the sack of Babylon in 1,595 BC. The gains were never consolidated and internecine struggles split the Hittite Old Kingdom, until the time came when it could be re-established by King Suppiluliumas I (1,380–1,346 BC). This resurgent Hittite empire reconquered the mountain tribes and principalities of Anatolia before beginning operations in Syria and northern Mesopotamia. This was Mitanni country, and the kings of Washukanni needed their allies now, more than ever before. Unfortunately, Egypt was paralysed by the social and religious trauma inflicted on it by Akhenaten, the son of Amenhotep III. Foreign affairs and military interventions were allowed to lapse, as the pharaoh relocated the court to a new cult city of Amarna. Worse still, a rival claimant to the Mitanni throne made alliances both with the Assyrians in the east and the Hittites in the west, leaving the king of Mitanni isolated. Even Babylon, now a great power that had become the equal of New Kingdom Egypt, would not help the Mitanni. The Hittite King Suppiluliumas I had cannily married his daughter to the king of Babylon in a diplomatic marriage that was designed to throw a ring around Mitanni.

Tutankhamun (1,333–1,323 BC), the young son of Pharaoh Akhenaten, made little if any impact on the affairs of Palestine and Syria, although his wife, Ankhesenamun, may have appeared briefly in the diplomatic records of the day. While a Hittite army led by Suppiluliumas I was besieging Carchemish, on the upper reaches of the Euphrates, the king received an emissary from the pharaoh's widow. The identity of this pharaoh is disputed, but it is most probably Tutankhamun and the queen is Ankhesenamun, his wife and half-sister. The message hints at her desperation in avoiding an imminent marriage to Ay, Tutankhamun's aged advisor and chamberlain: 'My husband has died and I have no son. They say that you have many sons. You might give me one of your sons, and he might become my husband'. Today, this dramatic letter is preserved in the Cairo Museum, a palm-sized clay tablet that is tucked into the corner of a shadowy wooden cabinet near the main entrance, it is dwarfed by the monumental statuary around it and overlooked by most of the visitors. The implications of this historic appeal could have radically changed Egyptian—and ancient—history, had a marriage been successfully arranged. Suppiluliumas did despatch one of his sons to Egypt, but he was murdered on the way and the throne was instead seized by Ay (1,323–1,319 BC). The Hittite king had other sons, however, and two of them were installed as kings of the newly conquered cities Carchemish and Aleppo.

When Mitanni eventually collapsed under the military and political pressures exerted upon it, the western part fell under the control of the Hittites, while the Assyrians captured the easternmost regions. The last vestiges of an independent Mitanni ended with the conquests of Assyrian King Shalmeneser I (1,273–1,244 BC). The Hittite empire stepped into the shoes of the Mitanni, dominating the

Near East 1300 BC

region of Syria and northern Mesopotamia with consummate skill both in diplomacy and in warfare.

Hatti was an empire made up of vassal states, such as Gasga, Wilusa, Kizzuwatna, and Kassiya, which were bound to the king by treaty. In war, these states contributed forces to the royal army and in return could expect help if attacked. Like the pharaoh, the Hittite king was the supreme commander of all military forces, although he could delegate that task to a trusted family member. Some of these princes and royal cousins would usually serve as provincial governors or garrison commanders. An axe-wielding royal guard, known as the *meshedi*, protected the king and his family, and in battle would have served as an elite chariot force.

Hittite forces were formidable in battle—their skills were honed by generations of warfare against mountain tribes and the warlike nations occupying the western half of Anatolia. Like other ancient kingdoms, though, Hittite armies relied on chariotry for much of their offensive power. Horse training and chariot driving had been learnt from the Hurrians, and, remarkably, a Hittite training manual was uncovered by archaeologists that proved to be a copy of a Hurrian original. A variety of chariot designs appear in Egyptian depictions of the Hittite forces at Kadesh, which is probably a reflection of the different regions that these contingents were drawn from. Most seem to have been of a robust design with their axles set more to the centre of the body than the rear, unlike Egyptian designs, and this philosophy was probably guided by the fact that each chariot carried a three-man crew consisting of a driver and two spearmen. Unlike the traditional *maryannu* form of chariot warfare, which utilised the vehicle as an archery platform, the Hittites excelled at the close combat attack. Enemy foot soldiers were engaged directly, running their chariot teams close into the infantry formations or directly against opposing chariots. Some of the crews are depicted in long scale coats of bronze.

Infantry formed a supporting arm and, like the chariot crews, they wore ankle-length robes, were clean shaven, and sported long pigtails. In one relief, Ramses II referred to the Hittite soldiers as *humty*, or 'women-warriors', presumably a reference to their unmanly locks. Preferred sidearms of these Hittite foot soldiers seem to have been axes and daggers. Units were organised according to a decimal system, with formations of ten, hundreds, and thousands of men and each was commanded by some member of the minor nobility.

The Battle of Kadesh

It was only a matter of time before Egypt and Hatti came to blows over affairs in Syria. With Washukkani destroyed, the Hittites began to campaign southwards, taking control of key cities that had previously owed allegiance to Mitanni. Like every great power, it encouraged dissension within cities that were currently allied with its southern rival, Egypt. Pharaoh Ay ruled for only four years and was succeeded first by his general, Horemheb (1,319–1,307 BC) and then by Ramses I, an ageing general who ruled only briefly, but whose name would come to dominate the Nineteenth Dynasty that he had established. Ramses' son, Seti I (1,305–1,290 BC), was, like his father, a military man and he led a bold campaign into Syria within the first year of his reign. Seti intended to restore the fortunes of Egyptian suzerainty abroad following what had become a long period of decline and instability.

Reliefs preserved on the outer north and east walls of the temple of Amun at Karnak record his victories. In many ways, these expeditions north followed the pattern set earlier in the New Kingdom, with a rapid march north along the 'Way of the Sea' securing the army's flank and its crucial supply lines from the seaports on the coast. It seems that the pharaoh had taken the opportunity to move against nomads that had migrated into Sinai; however, his ambitions lay much further north. In year two of his reign, Seti captured the city of Kadesh, an act of military provocation directed at the Hittite empire and its king, Muwatalis (1,315–1,296 BC). Before Seti could exploit this Syrian victory, he was recalled to Egypt in order to drive-out an incursion of Libyan tribes in the western Delta. In year four of the pharaoh's reign, a significant battle was fought between Seti's forces and the armies of Hatti. Although many Hittite soldiers were killed and large quantities of booty captured, there seems to have been little if any territorial gain. The Karnak reliefs claimed a great victory for Egypt, but in reality it was an uncomfortable peace that had been won and a peace that would not last for long. The Karnak reliefs depict bound Hittite soldiers being carried off to Egypt, while others are shown being ritually executed by the pharaoh himself. One of the reliefs at Karnak illustrates some of these prisoners obviously speaking words written for them by the Egyptian state:

> Chiefs of countries which knew not Egypt, which his majesty carried away from his victories in the country of Retenu-the-Wretched. They say, in magnifying his majesty and in acclaiming his victories: 'Hail to you! How great is your name, how mighty your power! The countries rejoice to be subject to you'.

At some point, the city of Kadesh must have fallen back into the hands of the Hittites because Seti's son, Ramses II (1,290–1,224 BC), famously fought to regain it in year five (1,286 BC) of his reign. Ramses inherited the throne at the age of twenty-five, although he had already ruled in partnership with his father for some time and had plenty of military experience. Pressure was on Ramses to emulate not just his father Seti I, but also those warrior-pharaohs that had made their mark on Egyptian history by securing their borders and conquering foreign lands.

A short, peremptory campaign was made in year four of his reign. A fourth army division (named Set) was mobilised for the first time and the Delta city of Piramesse was greatly expanded in order to serve as a supply base for the expedition. Ramses II's route through Palestine, in spring 1,287 BC, followed the time-honoured Way of the Sea and was marked by inscribed stelae set up at the ports of Tyre and Byblos. After turning east at Simyra, Ramses conquered the small kingdom of Amurru, which had recently switched its loyalty from that of Egypt to Hatti. With the security of his route in to Syria now secure, Ramses led the army back to Piramesse, where it would prepare for the recapture of Kadesh in the following spring.

Kadesh was a key location and one which had been fought over several times. It sat on a bend in the River Orontes and the waterway served the city as a natural defensive moat. The city itself dominated the southern end of the Syrian Plain and it had to be captured by the Egyptians before any war further north in Syria could be contemplated. What size force lay in wait for Ramses is uncertain, inscriptions on the walls of the temple of Amun at Karnak claim that the Egyptians faced off against 37,000 foot soldiers and upwards of 3,700 chariots. These may or may not reflect the actual troop strengths, yet there is no denying that the Hittite army gathering to defend Kadesh would certainly have been the largest that any pharaoh had yet faced. The four divisions of Egypt provided Ramses with a force roughly 20,000 strong, supplemented with a large number of mercenary troops and allied forces recruited from throughout Nubia, Palestine, Libya, and from the *Shardana*.

A royal prince reverses his sword to stab a Canaanite in the throat. Note his rounded shield slung across his back.

Marching out from Piramesse in late spring 1,287 BC, most of the Egyptian force turned inland after passing through Canaan to reach the Jordan valley. Meanwhile, a detachment of elite '*Ne'arin*' troops continued up the coast in order to secure the loyalty of the sea ports. It planned to rendezvous with Ramses and the main force further north. Ramses and his troops first passed Lake Galilee on the east and then the little town of Kumidi.

After having arrived at the ridge of Kadesh (the modern Kamu'at el-Harmel ridge), which afforded a view of the city to the north, the king captured two Shasu Bedouin who declared their loyalty to him. These scouts then informed Ramses that the Hittite army and its king, Muwatalis, were far away in Aleppo, some 180 km distant. This was indeed too good to be true; in fact, the Bedouin were working on behalf of the Hittites and had been sent into the Egyptian camp to deceive the pharaoh and his generals. Unaware that Muwatalis and his troops were stationed just to the east of Kadesh, Ramses crossed over the River Orontes at the ford of Shabtuna with his elite guards, his retainers, and the division of Amun, all still in marching order, unprepared for battle. They then began to set up camp on the north-western side of the city. Ramses was about to fall into a Hittite trap.

Egyptian guards soon captured two scouts, who were brought in front of Ramses for immediate interrogation:

> His majesty said to them: 'What are you?'
>
> They said: 'As for us, the ... ruler of the Hittites has sent us out to spy out where his majesty is'.
>
> Said his Majesty to them: 'Where is he, the ... ruler of Hatti? Behold, I have heard it say that he is in the land of Aleppo'.
>
> Said they: 'See, the ruler of Hatti is stationed, together with many countries which he has brought with him by force.... They are equipped with infantry and chariotry, bearing their weapons; more numerous are they than the sand of the shore. See, they are standing, drawn up for battle behind Kadesh the Deceitful'.
>
> Relief on the Battle of Kadesh, Thebes

Ramses urgently ordered his remaining three divisions to assemble; the division of Ra was the first to cross the River Orontes and it marched north to reach the Egyptian camp. At that moment, however, a force of Hittite chariots that had forded the river further north, swept down on the division, breaking up its formation and scattering the troops. This fast-moving chariot force then moved onto attack the division of Amun that was still setting up camp. Confusion reigned and Ramses found himself cut off and isolated. Nevertheless, he remained calm and was able to rally the chariots around him, defending the camp with repeated attacks on the Hittite force. The scene would have been chaotic and desperate, with clouds of dust kicked up by the turning chariots, Egyptian soldiers fleeing or defending, and Ramses leading his own counterattack. Total annihilation would have been certain but for the sudden and timely arrival of the elite guard unit that had planned to rendezvous with the Egyptian main force all along, the *Ne'arin*. Its seasoned troops and experienced commanders executed a devastating flank attack on the forces of King Muwatalis. Panic quickly spread through the Hittite soldiers and the army routed, scrambling desperately back across the Orontes.

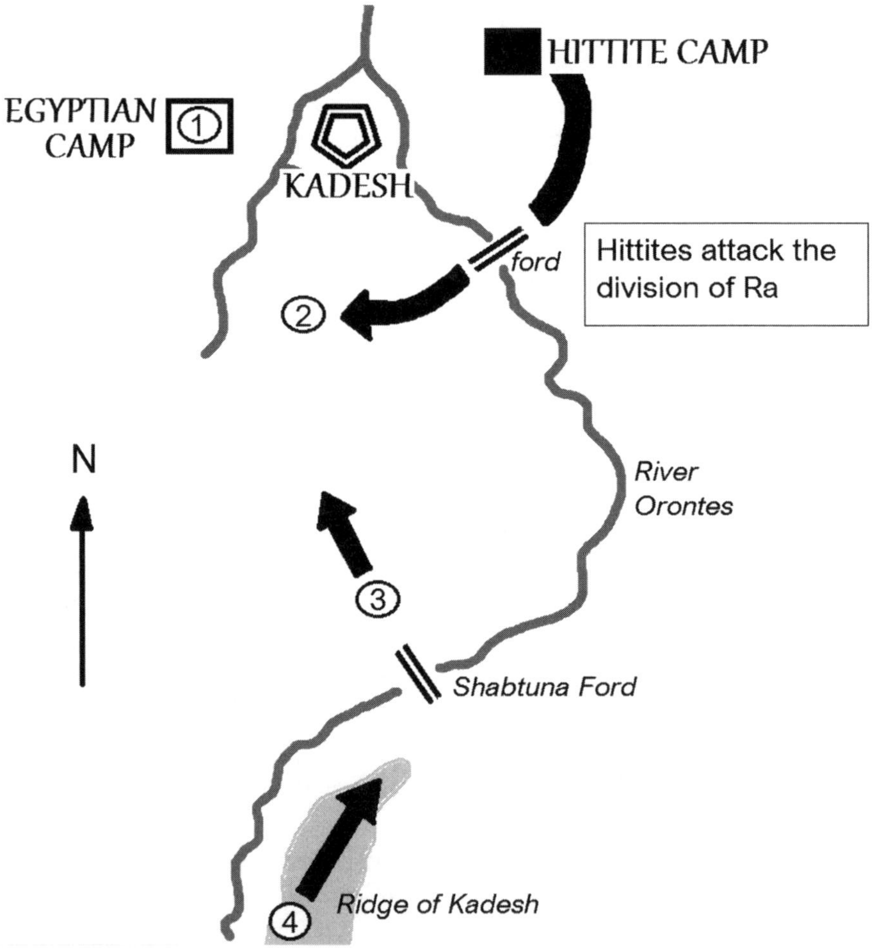

While the Egyptian division of Amun (1) made camp west of Kadesh, the rest of the divisions (2, Ra; 3, Ptah; 4, Set) follow on, all oblivious to the Hittite camp to the east. The division of Ra was then ambushed by a swift moving chariot squadron as it neared the city. Troops of Ra fled into their camp where Rameses II began a desperate counterattack, which successfully forced the Hittites back over the River Orontes.

In the aftermath of the battle, the final divisions of the Egyptian army, Ptah and Set, moved up to join their countrymen. In an attempt to exploit this unexpected victory, Ramses ordered a surprise attack of his own the next day; however, it failed to make any impact on the massed Hittite forces. A stalemate had been reached, with neither army able to defeat the other in a decisive manner. The battle, according to Ramses' own propaganda, had been an unequivocal victory against the Hittite empire. Yet there had been an agreement made in the immediate aftermath of Kadesh to end hostilities and to leave the territorial boundaries where they were. In the years that followed, Ramses II no longer sought out the Hittite army, although he did continue to campaign in Canaan and Amurru. In year twenty-one of his reign, almost two decades after the battle of Kadesh, Ramses II entered into a peace treaty with King Hattusilis III, the son and successor of Muwatalis. Perhaps the growing power of Assyria, on Hatti's eastern flank, forced the Hittite king to consider the possibility that Egypt and Assyria might form an alliance against him. To forestall this nightmare scenario, Hattusilis III despatched his daughter to Egypt, and her marriage to Ramses II sealed the agreement. Neither kingdom would encroach on the territories of the other, although, within fifty years, this issue would be moot. The Hittite empire was about to be overwhelmed and destroyed.

Sea Peoples

Ramses II had taken a number of auxiliary contingents with him to Kadesh, including Libyans, Nubians, and the enigmatic *Shardana*. These *Shardana* had come to the Egyptian Delta as raiders in 1,290 BC, but they were defeated and captured by the pharaoh. Impressed into military service, the *Shardana* fighters served Ramses well as an elite group of soldiers. In reliefs at Abydos that illustrate scenes from the Kadesh, the *Shardana* are shown as the pharaoh's personal bodyguard, as well as in battle killing fallen Hittite chariot crewmen. With their distinctive horned helmets, heavy body armour, and round shields, the *Shardana* brought a new weapon into the Egyptian armoury—they fought with straight, short swords. Another relief that depicts Ramses II's army besieging a Syrian city clearly shows *Shardana* with longswords. Conventionally, in Egyptology, these mercenaries originated from the island of Sardinia.

Following the death of Ramses II, Egypt entered a period of rapid decline that was hastened by a growing threat from aggressive war bands: 'northerners coming from all lands'. These invading armies repeatedly entered the Delta in an attempt to plunder or settle. While the Libyans, a perennial Egyptian foe, played a large part in some of these invasions, they introduced new mercenary groups into Egypt who would fight alongside them. Together, these numerous warrior bands are known as the 'Sea Peoples', following the reading of an inscription that recorded one pharaoh's victory against them:

> As for the foreign countries, they made a conspiracy in their sea-lands.... Removed and scattered in the fray were the lands at one time. No land could stand before their arms, from Hatti, Kode, Carchemish, Arzawa and Alashiya, (but they were) cut off at (one time).... Their confederation was the Peleset, Theker, Shekelesh, Denyen and Weshesh, lands united.
>
> Inscription of Ramses III at Medinet Habu

Much debate concerns the identity of these warlike adventurers; it was Emmanuel de Rougé who first coined the term 'Sea Peoples' ('*peuples de la mer Méditerranée*') and who suggested that their tribal names actually reflected their place of origin. Most of these proposed homelands lay in the Aegean or the western Mediterranean—the *Lukka*, *Tursha*, *Shardana*, *Shekelesh*, and *Ekwesh*, for example, would hail from Lycia, Tyrsenia, Sardinia, Sicily, and Greece respectively. The *Peleset* are equated with the Philistines of Biblical fame and as such can be located in southern Palestine. Some historians, including H. A. Ormerod, have shown some unease with de Rougé's conflation of place name with tribal name. Ormerod theorised that many of these peoples were not migrating tribes but mercenary bands from Anatolia. If correct, these opportunistic groups may have been borne out of the catastrophic collapse of the Hittite empire around 1,200 BC.

Whatever their actual origin, the Sea Peoples were part of a Bronze Age catastrophe that saw the destruction of the Mycenaean kingdom in Greece as well as the mighty Hittite empire and strong cities in Cyprus, in Syria, and in Palestine. New Kingdom Egypt, meanwhile, was able to mount a spirited defence against attacks by the Sea Peoples; nevertheless, it was to lose both its trade links and its prestige abroad. The kingdom of Egypt entered a rapid decline from which there would be no recovery.

Ramses II was succeeded by Merenptah (1,224–1,214 BC), one of his many sons. This pharaoh faced a large-scale Libyan invasion of the western Delta in his fifth year (1,220 BC).The desperate tribes brought their women, children, and cattle with them and were supported by armed bands of Sea Peoples. Following the defeat of the Sea Peoples and Libyans, military scribes counted 6,359 Libyan casualties, 742 *Tursha*, and around 200 dead from each of the tribes of *Ekwesh*, *Shekelesh*, and *Lukka*.

Thirty years later, a new dynasty was ruling Egypt and its second pharaoh, Ramses III (1,194–1,163 BC), faced an unprecedented series of foreign attacks on the Egyptian Delta. Like Merenptah, Ramses III fought off another large-scale invasion by Libyans and their Sea People allies. Reliefs carved on the walls of his well-preserved mortuary temple at Medinet Habu commemorate the pharaoh's victory in 1,190 BC. He had the trophy piles of hands and foreskins illustrated and the enemy casualty figures cut in stone above them. They

amounted to 12,535 enemy dead. Some six years later, in 1,184 BC, a second assault by Libyan settlers and their mercenary allies was made on the Delta. Again, Ramses III led a vigorous defence at the head of his New Kingdom army. The Libyan intention was to settle in the Delta—carvings of Libyan ox carts piled with belongings and accompanied by women and children make this clear.

Perhaps the most alarming of the invasions faced by Ramses III was a combined attack on the Delta by *Peleset* and *Tjekker* from Palestine, and *Shekelesh*, *Denyen*, and *Weshwesh* from the sea: 'They laid their hands upon the lands to the very circuit of the earth, their hearts confident and trusting: "Our plans will succeed."' This two pronged battle was fought by the Egyptian navy and army in 1,187 BC. The Egyptian army met the *Peleset* and *Tjekker* force in southern Palestine, soundly defeating them there. What exactly the plans of the enemy actually were is unknown, although the reliefs at Medinet Habu depict ox carts among the invading soldiers that carry goods and families. Did they intend to settle? Why? Both *Peleset* and *Tjekker* are referred to as 'Asiatics' in the inscriptions, a traditional appellation attached to Canaanites. Perhaps they were fleeing poor harvests and famine, or even social chaos and warfare that might have been caused by the collapse of the Hittite empire, further north.

Egyptian depictions of the different Sea Peoples often show distinct clothing, weaponry, and headgear. A common feature is the tasselled kilt, common at this period in southern Anatolia and the Levant. Armour worn by the warriors of

Detail from a relief at Medinet Habu that captures the Egyptian attack on the land invasion by the Sea Peoples and their allies. Wagons filled with belongings and family members are caught up in the melee. Here, *Shardana* mercenaries, fighting for Egypt, thrust their spears overarm and protect themselves with round shields. Note the longswords strapped to their chests.

the Sea Peoples has little in common with forms that had traditionally been seen in Hatti or the Levant; instead, the banded cuirass of either leather or bronze more resembles the heavy Dendra armour of bronze plates that was found in Mycenaean Greece. Medium-sized round shields are also common and the Sea Peoples seem to have routinely fought with either a spear or a bronze longsword. Some individuals wear short swords strapped to their chests. Reliefs also portray the different groups of raiders wearing their own styles of headgear, from turbans to caps and helmets sporting horns to elaborate headdresses topped with crowns of either horsehair, leather strips, or reeds. These depictions are not unique; a column of infantrymen decorates the so-called Warrior Vase found by Heinrich Schliemann within the citadel of Mycenae, in Greece. Dated to around 1,200 BC, roughly contemporaneous with the reign of Ramses III and his struggles with the Sea Peoples, it shows soldiers with rounded shields marching in step with spears over their shoulders. They wear metal or padded greaves on their shins and heavy armour shirts, both made of either padded linen or, more likely, of bronze. On their heads, they wear helmets topped with a pair of horns. They big question that cannot be satisfactorily answered is: are these soldiers Sea Peoples as recorded by Mycenean potters or are they Mycenean warriors that were recorded by Egyptian stonemasons as Sea Peoples?

Although some Sea Peoples are depicted fighting from chariots in the land battle of 1,187 BC, the bulk of the Sea Peoples fought as infantrymen. Historian Robert Drews believes that this new invention—that of the heavily armed foot soldier equipped with the latest bronze sword and a general-purpose round shield—revolutionised ancient warfare. The existence of these swordsmen may well have rendered the chariot tactics of the day impotent, and may even have triggered the collapse of so many Near Eastern palace states at this time.

Despite the twin victories of Ramses III and the glorious throne name that he had adopted in order to associate his reign with that of Ramses II (known to history with justification as Ramses the Great), the Egyptian empire fell away. The *Peleset* settled in Palestine and there was nothing the pharaoh could do about it—easy overland access to Lebanon and Syria had vanished and so too had the familiar politics of the Levant.

Ramses III had been the second pharaoh of the Twentieth Dynasty. During the next ninety years, there would be eight more kings calling themselves Ramses and all were descended from Ramses III. Palestine had been lost, however, and control of Nubia was also lost by the end of the dynasty. Temples and priesthoods slowly began to assume the government of Upper Egypt as the power of the Egyptian throne waned. Civil war and rival centres of power split Egypt, bringing an end to the Twentieth Dynasty and the New Kingdom. Economically, the kingdom was virtually bankrupt, its prestige abroad was destroyed, and bigger and better empires were flexing their muscles throughout the region. Egypt suffered repeated invasions, and over the next few centuries, she was ruled by Nubian and Libyan dynasties, as well as the forces of Assyria, Persia, Macedonia, and, ultimately, those of Rome.

6

A Soldier's Lot

When he dies at the edge of the desert there is no one to perpetuate his name.
For him, both life and death are [equally] painful.

Satire of the Trades

Scribes of the New Kingdom often denigrated the soldier and his role in order to dissuade potential scribes from straying into the military realm, yet accounts of some career soldiers attest to the army's great rewards. It is clear from the surviving biographies of Egyptian military officers (like Ahmose, son of Ebana, writing at the beginning of the New Kingdom) that individuals gained a great deal of pride from their service in the army. They are at pains to list their awards and the prizes captured in battle, and they record in glowing tones both their promotions and the prestigious assignments given to them.

Army life in the New Kingdom was both profitable and prestigious—at least for some. These accounts are written by career soldiers, men whose fathers had seen military service; they were part of the hereditary military class that now dominated the upper echelons of New Kingdom government. A retiring soldier left his position to his son, who followed in his father's footsteps. Along with the position came any land, slaves, and other benefits that went with it. Much of this had probably been 'won' by the retired veteran during his service with the army abroad. With land to farm, a modest, but comfortable house, and slaves to minister to the needs of the family, the veteran and his comrades were part of a new 'middle class' of small and medium-sized property owners, the like of which Egypt had not seen before. Sandwiched somewhere between the ruling class and the workers, the hereditary soldiers became gentlemen farmers, with land that they did not technically own, farmed by tenants for both benefit and profit.

Veterans writing about their exploits seem to display a keen sense that they are playing their part within Egyptian history, they are not simply following orders or currying favour with the 'top brass'. These soldiers are also being publicly rewarded for their courage and several of the accounts allude to a personal relationship with the pharaoh. Here we see the soldiery relating to the pharaoh as a comrade-in-arms, as one who shares the travails of the battlefield and who rewards those who display bravery in his presence.

The officer Amenemhab fought with Tuthmosis III in Asia and many years later was one of the rowers on the royal barge. The pharaoh's son, Amenhotep II, was king at that time, but he recognised Amenemhab:

> I know you from the time when I was in the nest, when you were a companion of my father. I now appoint you lieutenant of the army, and from now on you will command the royal bodyguard.
>
> Biography of Amenemhab, written on the walls of his tomb

Advancement and success within the military hierarchy was possible for any man, should he be bold enough, valiant enough, and lucky enough.

Preparation for War

Now larger, more active, and more professionally run than its Middle Kingdom equivalent, the New Kingdom army required a well-trained and permanent military force. Fresh recruits (*nefru*) were typically young farmers who were used to a tough, outdoor life-style; most would have been in their late teens at the time of recruitment. The officer responsible for raising these troops for Pharaoh was the Scribe of Recruits:

> My lord again showed favour to me; the King of Upper and Lower Egypt (Amenhotep III), he put all the people subject to me, and the listing of their number under my control, as superior king's-scribe over recruits. I levied the (military) classes of my lord, my pen reckoned the numbers of millions.... I placed troops at the heads of the ways to turn back the foreigners in their places. The Two Lands were surrounded with a watch, scouting for the Sand-dwellers. I did likewise at the heads of the river mouths, which were closed under my troops, except to the troops of the royal marines.'
>
> Inscription of Amenhotep son of Hapi

A measure of the standing enjoyed by the Scribe of Recruits can be had when one considers that Horemheb (1,319–1,307 BC), the general who fought for Tutankhamun, his father Akhenaten, and their vizier Ay, had once occupied the post of Scribe of Recruits. He rose to fill the vacuum left by their deaths and became the final pharaoh of the Eighteenth Dynasty.

Training and deployment would have been conducted at one of the major military centres of Egypt, either at Memphis or Thebes (and later at Piramesse). Here they were taught how to march within a drill company (*sekheperu*), how to fight with the weapons of the day, and how to block the attacks of an enemy with a shield. On the walls of the tomb of Userhat, who served as a military officer during the reign of Amenhotep II, conscripts are shown sat on the ground having their heads shaved while a quartermaster issues rations. Some of the festivals and other celebrations that are depicted on New Kingdom wall paintings include 'stick fights', where pairs of combatants duel with wooden staves. Some of these fighters wear protective guards lashed to their vulnerable forearms. From the tomb of Amenmose, we know that these men are soldiers. Two stick-fighter taunt one another, with hieroglyphic inscriptions that accompany the scene. 'Be watchful you wretched, boastful soldier', shouts one, while his opponent replies dismissively, 'It is you who is a fool to lay a hand on one of his majesty's soldiers!' It is likely that this Egyptian 'sport' formed part of the non-lethal training regime of young recruits.

In a similar vein, on the walls of the tomb of Kheruef at Thebes, soldiers are shown engaging in boxing matches. Wrestling soldiers are also commonly depicted elsewhere. It is easy to see how these aggressive sports would form an essential part of a recruit's initial training. Since archery formed such an

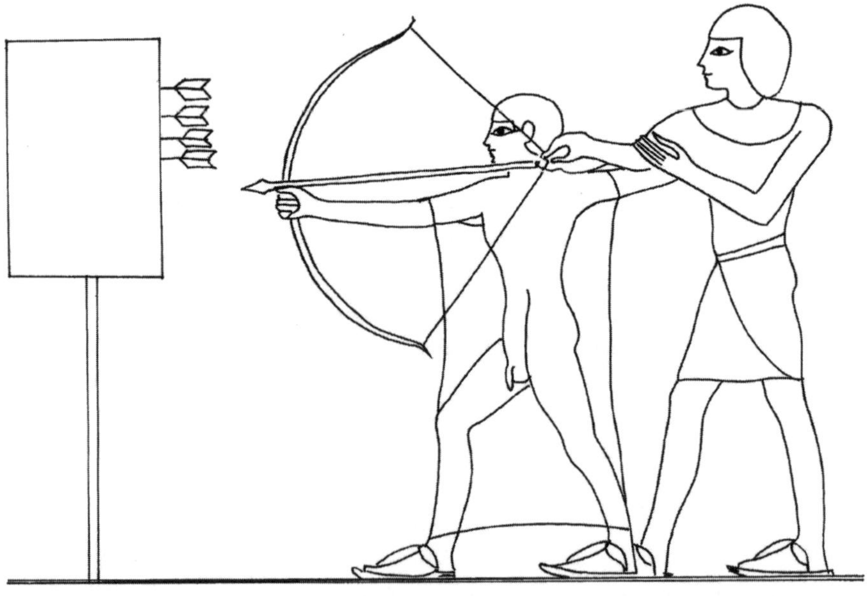

Theban tomb painting that depicts a recruit undergoing archery training. The instructor guides him from behind.

important part of Egyptian military doctrine, it is not surprising that we find scenes of young recruits being taught how to shoot the composite bow. In some, the archery instructor stands behind his charge, directing him and giving advice on his technique or his stance. 'Pull the line to your ear,' says one, 'Keep strong your arms. Act with force and strength.'

A key part of military training is the instilling of discipline, and despite the scribal prejudice against life in the army, the Miscellanies give us a taste of this ancient discipline:

> [The recruit] is thrashed to exhaustion. He awakens in the morning only to receive beatings until he is split open with wounds. He is equipped with weapons upon his arm, he is standing on the drill field every day. A painful blow is given to his body, a powerful blow is given to his body, a powerful blow upon his head, his eyes and his nose.

Seasoned veteran soldiers who had several years of service under their belt became known by the term *menfyt*. As in the Old and Middle Kingdoms, soldiers within the army divisions of the New Kingdom were put to work during peaceful times with duties to escort mining expeditions into foreign lands and to assist in the transportation of stone blocks and statues where additional manpower was needed. A myriad of other tasks were foisted upon the troops, including the tracking of escaped prisoners with dogs and the escort of state dignitaries into neighbouring kingdoms. Just as today, a logistics train followed these army units and military scribes were there at every stage to keep records and to disburse rations and supplies as needed.

Marching to War

A hierarchy of military scribes paralleled the standard combat formations, and these scribes were embedded in every level of the division. Companies (*sa*), hosts (*pedjet*), divisions (*mesha*), garrisons, and fortresses all had military scribes on staff who maintained the duty rosters and supply lists that any sophisticated army must rely on. Providing food, water, clothing, medicines, tools, weapons, and all of the other consumables and equipment for a column of soldiers would have been a difficult task. When that column has to cross the deserts of Sinai and Negev, this task became formidable. Logistics were discussed in Chapter 3, here we are concerned with the soldier's lot—what was he carrying on the march? What was the experience like for these men who marched hundreds of kilometres in baking temperatures to fight at the end of it?

A military scribe named Hori wrote a satirical letter to a colleague of his that has survived to give us a rare snapshot of how Egyptian infantryman were sometimes treated on the march. The letter questions the skills and abilities of a fellow scribe named Amenemope and throws a problem at him:

> The troops that are before you number 1,900: 520 Shardana, 1,600 Qehaq (Libyans), 100 Meshwesh (Libyans), 880 Nubians—5,000 in all, not counting their officers. A present is brought before you of bread, livestock, wine. The number of men is too great for you and the victuals are insufficient for them.... The soldiers are numerous and the victuals few.... The army is prepared and ready. Register them quickly, each according to his troop. The Bedouin are watching furtively: 'What a cunning scribe!' (in Syriac, in the text) they say. Midday has arrived and the camp is hot. [The Egyptian soldiers] say: 'It is time to go. Do not anger the troop officer! We have a long march ahead of us'. But, let us say it, why is there no bread at all? Or night quarters are far away. Good lord, what does it mean to ill treat us in this way? Yet you are an intelligent scribe.
>
> *Anastasi Papyrus I*

Here we get the sense of a large detachment, perhaps on patrol, under surveillance by the very people they are there to fight, far from the regular supply lines. British soldiers in Forward Operating Bases (FOBs) and patrol bases at Sangin, Musa Qala, or Nad Ali in Afghanistan's Helmand province must have had similar gripes about food, long patrols, and the realisation that the Taliban had them under surveillance.

Night quarters might have been a billet in a friendly city or, more likely, a military camp within the shadow of an allied city-state. Wall carvings from the city of Amarna depict soldiers sleeping beneath blankets, which must have been part of their personal kit. Soldiers could keep themselves warm during the cold desert nights with a campfire, as a carving in the Brooklyn Museum shows; in it, three men stand close to a fire while a comrade fans the flames.

Tents were certainly used by some members of the army, as depictions of Ramses II's camp at Kadesh show. There are a number of reliefs that illustrate the Battle of Kadesh and there are two in particular that depict the temporary camp set up by Ramses' soldiers outside Kadesh. One is on the west wing of the Luxor temple pylon and the other is on the north wall of the Great Temple at Abu Simbel. These remarkably detailed scenes provide a view of the Egyptian camp under assault from Hittite chariot troops. The camp is rectangular, and two large tented pavilions have been pitched in the centre for Ramses and his staff. The smaller, cylindrical tents of his officers surround this central encampment. Around the perimeter of the camp, on an earthen rampart, stands a defensive palisade of infantry shields; they are locked together to provide a defined boundary. One of the shield walls of Ramses' camp is cut by a gap, a gateway to allow entry, and the artist has added detail that suggests some kind of wooden gate.

Gateway to a military encampment, guarded by soldiers armed with staves and swords. The perimeter wall of shields is seen on a number of other military reliefs.

The tents were almost certainly reserved for the officer corps and appear cylindrical in shape with conical roofs, similar to a stereotypical knight's jousting tent. Inside they contain small tables, cooking paraphernalia, and stools. Such tents were made of linen canvas rather than the heavy goat-leather tents used by the much later Roman legions. Their elite occupants were attended by servants, slaves, and bodyguards, although doctors, cooks, and scribes would also have attended the officers, both junior and senior. Egyptologist Bridget McDermott has suggested that traders, doctors, scribes, cooks, metal workers, and female servants routinely followed the army on campaign, but she has also postulated the idea that women were employed as prostitutes for the benefit of the soldiers. Camp followers like this were a common feature of ancient warfare. Children are often shown attending soldiers in scenes of daily life, which makes their presence on campaign a likelihood. Reliefs show that the routine of daily life continued within Ramses' marching camp; asses are being unloaded, people are busy washing themselves, and so on.

An age-old literary tradition used by scribes to denigrate other careers and emphasise or exaggerate their hardships was used as a recruiting tool. Scribes, the men who ordered ancient Egyptian society, considered their profession to be far superior to all others. A number of these 'recruiting texts' have survived and some take a special delight in underlining the difficulties, dangers, and frustrations experienced by that great rival to the scribal career—the soldier.

Are these satires in any way accurate or are they fabrications? As we have already seen, many scribes accompanied the army on campaign, witnessing first-hand the travails of the common foot soldier. The texts provide flavourful details that certainly tally with the experiences of many other soldiers from pre-modern armies. We should not discount these scribal advertisements, but instead interpret them as worst case scenarios, terrible experiences suffered by soldiers *in extremis*—but realistic and viable nonetheless.

One of the most evocative of these satirical texts is the *Papyrus Lansing*, dated to the late New Kingdom and written by the royal scribe and chief overseer of cattle Nebmare-nakht for his apprentice, the scribe Wenemdiamun:

> Come, let me describe to you the ills of the soldier, since his superiors are many: the general, the chief of archers, the *seket*-officer who is before them, the standard-bearer, the lieutenant, the [military] scribe, the commander of fifty men, the garrison chief. They come and go from the halls of the palace of the king and say: 'Let them work'.
>
> He is woken in the early hours of the morning. They attach themselves to his ribs as to an ass, and he works from dawn to sunset, in the darkness of the night. He is hungry; his body is tormented; he is dead while still alive. He receives his ration of corn when he is released from his duties, but when it is ground it is no longer good.
>
> He is recalled into Syria before he has rested. There are neither clothes nor sandals. The arms of war have been gathered together at the fortress of Tjalu.
>
> His hill marches are long, he drinks water once every three days, and it is fetid and tastes of salt. His body is destroyed by dysentery. The enemy comes and surrounds him with arrows; life is far from him. They say: 'Come on, brave soldier, win yourself a glorious name!' But he no longer knows who he is. His body is weak and his knee contemptible before [the enemy]. Victory takes place. The booty destined for Egypt is assigned to His Majesty. The foreign woman [prisoner] is taken by a fainting fit during the march and placed on the shoulders of the soldier. His shoulder bag is abandoned and taken by others, because he is loaded down by the prisoner. His wife and children are in their village. But he dies before reaching them.
>
> If he survives, he is destroyed by marching. Whether in quarters or in the country, he is discontent. If he runs and goes away with the deserters, all of his people are imprisoned. When he dies at the edge of the desert, there is no one to perpetuate his name. For him both life and death are [equally] painful.

Nebmare-nakht's account of the soldier's trials provides some interesting details that we would not otherwise be aware of. He has a shoulder bag, into which he would put his rations, personal belongings, and any booty he might be able to capture for himself. The *Papyrus Anastasi III* corroborates this, with the statement that 'his bread and water are carried on his shoulders like a donkey's burden. His neck becomes calloused'. Cuts, callouses, and burn marks on the side of the neck are a common facet of long-distance marching when carrying kit bags, waterskins, and shields slung over one shoulder or another, as the author's personal experience in recreating and testing the marching kit of Roman legionaries can attest. A soldier's marching pack can be seen in some of the scenes depicting the military camp at Kadesh—it took the form of a stick, at the end of which a small linen kit-bag was tied.

Papyrus Lansing also tells us that the soldiers were given their ration of wheat as a grain, not as flour, and that they would be expected to grind it themselves. This implies the existence of portable grindstones within the Egyptian camp that were probably shared between a squad. The grindstones of this era were saddle querns, where a top stone was rubbed repeatedly over grain in a backwards and forwards motion—they are illustrated on a relief from the tomb-chapel of Hetepherakht. Clothes and sandals are mentioned with the implication that these items should have been provided for him, but our soldier has neither. A few of the soldiers in the reliefs and carvings of the great monuments are shown wearing sandals and the papyrus suggests that they were certainly something that a soldier should ordinarily have. The lid and panels of a chest that was found among King Tutankhamun's burial goods was decorated with paintings of his royal guard and most of these soldiers wear sandals.

Finally, it is interesting to note the presence in the narrative of a slave girl, a prisoner taken (or awarded) as a prize in battle. Where Ahmose, son of Ebana, fighting at Avaris against the Hyksos, had proudly boasted that the pharaoh had presented him with one male and three female slaves, *Papyrus Lansing* turns the glory of the prize on its head. The girl cannot cope with the tough rigours of the march, and in order to retain this trophy, he must abandon his kit bag and carry her over his shoulder. This presents us with a more rounded and down-to-earth portrayal of slave ownership.

Food and Clothing

In the New Kingdom, military scribes formed the backbone of an efficient logistical organisation that attempted to supply the troops with everything they needed, wherever they were based. We know that soldiers were routinely supplied with bread, livestock, grain, linen, and ointment.

Food, or the lack of it, has always been of paramount importance to the soldier in every age, whether he was an Egyptian, Roman, Assyrian, British Red Coat, or American GI. The Middle Kingdom fortresses of Nubia have shed some light on how the disbursement of rations was managed. At the frontier fort of Uronarti, a number of wooden tallies in the shape of different types of loaf were handed out to troops for use as bread-ration tokens. This does not contradict the *Papyrus Lansing*, which mentioned a ration of grain, since the Roman army also provided bread or hardtack to its troops at times and wheat grains at others. Obviously bread was more suited to the environment of the Egyptian garrison, or the frontier fort, since it had to be eaten relatively quickly and was too bulky to carry on the march. Wheat or barley grains (both were grown in ancient Egypt, with the poorer households eating more barley bread than wheat) did not spoil easily and could be ground up for their wheat content months after they were issued. Tomb scenes often show bags of grain being bartered for everyday goods, and we can safely assume that the troops received their grain ration in similar linen bags.

Loaves were typically flat and unleavened, much like the Greek pitta or Indian naan. They were often shaped as triangles, ovals, or indented squares. Flatbreads like this were baked either in the ashes of a fire, on a flat stone by the fireside, within a clay oven, or slapped onto the outside of a pottery oven. Bread was also baked in pre-made conical moulds; these types of loaves are commonly depicted as offerings within tombs. The Egyptians called this 'festival bread', and thousands of fragments of clay mould were discovered at el-Amarna—dated to the Eighteenth Dynasty. Ash cakes, bread simply baked in the hot ashes of a camp fire, will have fed the soldiers when on campaign, since this flatbread requires neither bread oven nor bread mould. Mesopotamian soldiers at this time were eating bread baked in just this fashion, and they took great pride in their humble fare. Careful analysis of bread that has survived within burial chambers has discovered that grit and sand was a common unwanted ingredient of ancient Egyptian bread, either from the grind stone itself or simply from wind-blown sand. A diet of this gritty Egyptian bread led to the wearing down of tooth enamel, which inevitably led to the development of painful and life-threatening abscesses.

Some breads were flavoured with dates, egg, milk, honey, fruit, animal fat, or cumin seeds, but these types of bread must have been a luxury for the soldier on the march. Other foods eaten by the Egyptian poor, and therefore good candidates for the military diet, include garlic, onions, radishes, meloukhia leaves (a member of the hemp family), leeks, and cucumber. The cucumber could have been easily pickled to extend its 'shelf-life'. Chick peas, lentils, and broad beans were also staple foods—the modern bean dish called fūl has a long pedigree, and is cooked overnight in an earthenware pot in the ashes of the day's fire. It is flavoured with garlic, fresh herbs, oil, and spices, and, when eaten, is usually accompanied by plain bread, fish (either salted or sun-dried), or boiled eggs. Meat of any sort would have been a rare treat for the soldier.

Wine was part of the ration, although we should not imagine this to resemble the international wines with which we are familiar today; Egyptians not only made wine from the grape harvest, but also (according to later Roman writer and naturalist Pliny) from plums, pomegranates, dates, and figs. Large quantities of beer were drunk by Egyptians of all classes and the fermentation of yeast went hand-in-hand with the baking of bread. Beer was a nutritious drink, and although most families brewed their own, professional brewers would have produced beer to an industrial level for the soldiers.

A number of estimates have been made concerning the amount and type of rations carried on the march by ancient armies. Many estimate the energy requirements for an adult male of this period to be around 3,300 calories, roughly equating to 1.36 kg of grain (or its nutritional equivalent) each day. The most useful of these estimates was made by Barry Kemp in 1986, following a 1917 report on modern Egyptian prison conditions. In it, 1,800 calories were needed for subsistence, 2,200 for no work, 2,800 for light work, and 3,200 for a day of hard labour. A full division of troops would therefore need to carry, forage, or collect from pre-positioned caches 6,800 kg of grain or its equivalent. Pharaohs often planned their campaigns well ahead of time and it had become routine to cache supplies along the Way of Horus and at friendly city-states dotted throughout Palestine. Army rations were carried on the backs of donkeys, either in clay jars, sacks, or baskets woven from papyrus stem.

Desert crossings also required the army to carry a supply of water, and a 5,000-strong division would need to drink around 11,000 litres of water per day. This assumes a daily requirement of 2.2 litres per man. From inscriptions from the temple of Redesiyeh, Seti I stated: 'How evil is the way without water!' When Pharaoh Merenptah routed a Libyan invasion in his fifth year, an account of the event was recorded on a stela from the pharaoh's mortuary temple:

> The archers threw down their bows and the heart of their fleet-ones was weary with marching. They loosed their water skins and threw them to the ground, their bags were taken and thrown out.

In garrison, the soldiers cooked their food on a simple outdoor hearth formed from a wide-dished pot set into the floor. The fire was started with a bow drill and, once alight, was fanned with a palm or papyrus leaf. In a landscape with little easily collected firewood, fuel for the fire consisted of dried animal dung, straw, small branches of acacia or tamarisk, or palm leaves. Cook pots were of unglazed Nile clay and larger examples had looped handles for suspending over the fire.

Soldiers in the New Kingdom are typically depicted wearing a short linen kilt made of undyed white linen—no other clothes are worn. The kilt seems to be a larger form of the triangular 'under-over' loincloth, where the wide straight edge ties around the waist and the triangle of fabric passes between the legs to then feed up and underneath the waist tie at the front, with the apex of the triangle then hanging down between the thighs. A stack of linen loincloths was discovered inside the tomb of Kha, an architect of the mid-Eighteenth Dynasty, at Deir-el Medina. They seem typical of the small linen loincloths

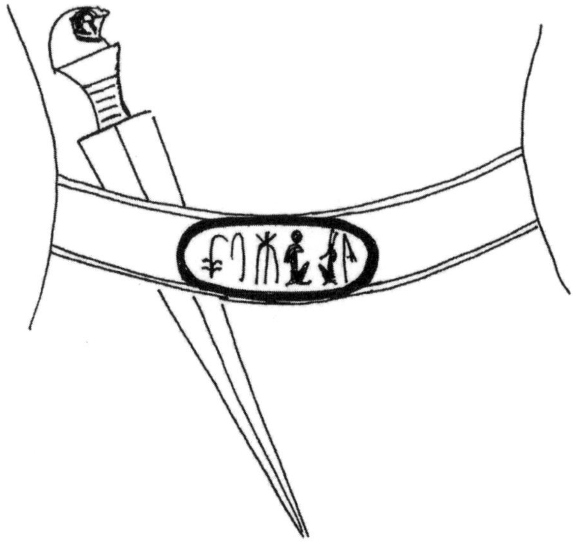

Method of carrying a short sword, tucked inside a decorated waist belt.

worn by most male Egyptians, and the military kilts of the New Kingdom were larger-scale versions.

Some Egyptologists have interpreted the triangular 'tongue' of the kilt that hung down from the waist as a solid piece of linen, perhaps of many layers glued together—this would have served as a 'groin guard'. Although there are a number of reliefs (such as those of Ramses III at Medinet Habu) that do indeed seem to show such a solid piece of kit, many others depict what is obviously a simple triangle of hanging linen. The idea of a solid half-metre board hanging from the waist is ludicrous to anyone who has spent any time recreating the marching practices of ancient soldiers over long distances and varied terrains (and the author is one of these). A large shield slung on the back or carried in the left hand over rough terrain is trouble enough, but the prospect of an inflexible, triangular-shaped, shield-like groin guard banging against the legs at every step and restricting the soldier's ability to step up over rocks or other obstacles cannot be seriously entertained.

There were other types of kilt worn by different troop types at different periods of New Kingdom history. Most of the Egyptian archers and all chariot troops are often shown in long, ankle-length skirts, and some of these soldiers instead wore full-length short-sleeved robes. Some of the Egyptian marines, shown on the walls of the temple of Medinet Habu fighting the Sea Peoples, wear the native dress of their enemies. This was a short wrap-around kilt, probably made of linen and with wide bands or strips that may indicate leather reinforcement. Sea Peoples were known to have fought within the ranks of the

Egyptian army in the Later New Kingdom, and this adoption of foreign garb perhaps reflects this multi-ethnic mix of fashions. Note that few soldiers are shown wearing sandals.

Over the basic loincloth-style kilt there are some troops, usually sailors and marines, who wear an open-work style slit-leather garment. This so-called 'naval kilt' may have protected the linen kilt from the rough treatment it received on campaign life. The naval kilt was cut from a single piece of leather, and although pierced by many open-work slits, a solid panel was left intact at the rear where a rower might sit on the wooden bench of a warship. A well-preserved example of a naval kilt is held in the British Museum collection.

A new type of headwear among soldiers, the striped headcloth, became popular during the Nineteenth and Twentieth (or 'Ramesside') Dynasties. This headcloth closely resembled the striped *nemes* headdress worn by Egyptian pharaohs from the Old Kingdom onwards, made famous by the gold death mask of Tutankhamun. It covered the crown and back of a soldier's head and flared out at the base of the neck. Why were the troops wearing these *nemes*-like headcloths now?

Pharaohs of the Nineteenth Dynasty were soldiers—both Ramses I and Seti I had served as senior army commanders before becoming king of Egypt. Their successors led from the front and they elevated the status of the army and that of the common soldier to much greater levels than in previous dynasties. In a similar manner, Roman emperors in the third century AD fought desperately to keep the empire together and spent months in the field with their troops, away from Rome. Retaining the loyalty of the common legionary was crucial, and many emperors of the period dressed like their men and shared the same rations; Caracalla (AD 188–217) marched on foot beside his men and even made a show of grinding his own wheat ration. In this, the soldier-emperors were sharing the hardships of the legions in an attempt to gain their respect and their loyalty. By allowing the common Egyptian soldiers to wear the *nemes*-style headcloth, pharaohs of the Nineteenth Dynasty may have been working in a similar fashion to Roman emperors like Caracalla—bringing common soldier and head of state together

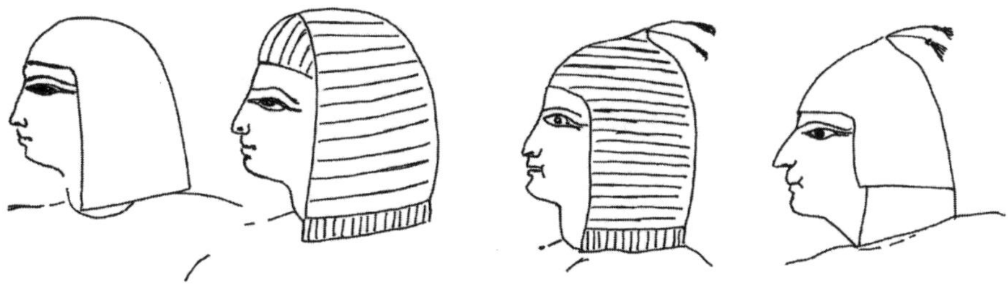

Examples of military headcloths, worn by Egyptian soldiers during the Nineteenth Dynasty.

to foster loyalty. Allowing regular soldiers to wear a facsimile of the *nemes* headdress may represent a boon or honour—the pharaoh was sharing some of his own status with the soldiers that the Egyptian state had now come to depend on.

Armour

In ancient warfare, the shield is king; from behind it, a warrior could strike out at his foe while protecting his body from a simultaneous counterblow. Many weapons, including spears, axes, and most bronze blades, were not capable of parrying the blows of an attacker. Even then, during the heat of battle, a soldier did not fight alone, but in massed ranks. He may have faced attacks from several opponents simultaneously, and in this regard, the shield proved a lifesaver. Armour, meanwhile, came late to Egyptian warfare. From reliefs of the Old and Middle Kingdoms, there are few depictions of helmets or body armour. Armour was a passive defence, it was back-up protection designed to reduce injury and wounding for that moment when an attack got past the shield parry or weapon block.

Scale Armour

Ironically, it was not the cheap, easily produced body armour of the foot soldier that first emerged onto the Egyptian battlefield; instead, the first examples of personal protection were the long coats of bronze scale (*tiryana*) worn by chariot-warriors. The reasons are clear: when the composite bow and the chariot took centre stage on the battlefield, some mechanism had to be found to protect the vulnerable driver and the elite chariot warrior. Both of these soldiers required their hands free, one to hold the reins and control the horses, the other to load and shoot the bow. The Hittites famously developed a three-man crew that included a dedicated shield-bearer who could protect both the warrior and himself. Early New Kingdom pharaohs followed the Mitanni model, where the crews were protected by long, expensive coats of bronze scale. Reasonably light in weight, flexible, and fairly resistant to fast-moving arrows, the bronze scale coat was provided to many of the Egyptian chariot crews of the New Kingdom. Not all crews were so well armoured, no kingdom had the resources to outfit all of its chariot soldiers in this fashion, not even pharaonic Egypt.

The Theban tomb of the nobleman Kenamun included a detailed painting of a coat of scale armour. It would have reached the wearer's knees and its arms were short (reaching perhaps to the elbow). This matches depictions of Canaanite chariot armour on a relief dedicated to a victory won by Tuthmosis IV. Both the battle relief and the Kenamun shirt show a type of solid neck ring, which protected that vulnerable area. The early date of the tomb painting and its likeness to the Tuthmosis IV armour suggests that it actually depicts a coat of

Canaanite scale that had been imported from Syria or Palestine. We know that traffic of this sort occurred throughout the history of the New Kingdom—when Amenhotep III received the daughter of King Tushratta of Mitanni as his wife, the girl was accompanied by wedding gifts that included horses and chariot equipment, helmets, shields, and bronze scale coats. Military necessity quickly drove the Egyptian armourers to develop scale armour of their own.

The scales and the neck guard on the Kenamun painting were coloured yellow to give them the appearance of bronze, and, using some basic extrapolation, was made up of 450 individual scales sewn onto a blue linen tunic that acted as a backing cloth. Inventories of military equipment within the northern Mesopotamian archives of Nuzi make it clear that scales came in two sizes: 'large' and 'small'. These are listed separately—coats could be made of large or small scales or a mixture of both. For example, one scale coat is described as being constructed of 680 scales (280 small and 400 large). Another coat is listed as containing 1,035 scales, which indicates how diverse and of varying quality these pieces of armour were, not just from kingdom to kingdom, but even within a single workshop. Generally, however, the more scales and the smaller the scales were in size, the better the protection it provided.

Each scale had been cut from a sheet of bronze and had holes drilled through several edges, usually along the top and bottom edges and one side. It was through these holes that the individual scale was stitched to the backing fabric with linen thread. Scales recovered from excavations throughout the Near East and those depicted in such detail on the walls of Kenamun's tomb have a centrally raised spine, which provided each scale with enhanced strength against a potential arrow strike. Bronze scales were discovered within the tomb of Amenhotep III and some of the cloth onto which they were attached still survived.

The author has worn a scale coat for extended periods and spent a good deal of time with the expert craftsman who made it. Compared to ringmail (also known as chainmail) that was common to much later historical periods, the scale coat was certainly lighter and easier to wear. Unlike chainmail shirts, however, which can be put on like some over-sized T-shirt, the scale coat has a side-opening and is fastened together with leather straps and bronze buckles. The opening on the modern reconstruction had been located on the left-hand side of the coat, which is the wearer's shield side; this, of course, mitigated the weakness at this point. After many days of use, the main disadvantage of the reproduction scale coat became clear: it required continual maintenance. Threads snapped and scales came loose. Scales also became snagged on straps or other items of equipment, ripping them loose or bending them out of shape. This kind of damage was most severe when the author wore the scale coat on cross-country marches, testing the armour 'in the field' as it were. Caught quickly, none of this damage was difficult to repair, but it was time consuming and required a supply of spare scales and thread.

Helmets

Helmets were not a common item of military hardware within the Egyptian army. When they did appear, it was in tandem with the charioteer's scale coat, and, like the scale coat, helmets followed the Mitanni pattern. They were high-crowned, bronze helmets without cheek pieces or neck guards—many featured small crests or ostrich feathers. In their native lands, they were known as *gurpisu siparri*, and may have reached the Nile valley, like the scale armour, as tribute from conquered cities throughout the Near East. A number of Theban tombs, including those of Rekhmire, Menkheperrasonb, and Amenmose, show these helmets stacked on shelves or being carried on trays. They were prized objects, stored within elaborate helmet boxes and sought after as tribute or on the battlefield as booty.

Much more close-fitting versions of this helmet appear in reliefs from the reign of Pharaoh Horemheb (1,319–1,307 BC), but the troops depicted are infantrymen. Like the *gurpisu siparri*, these foot soldiers' helmets were probably made of bronze or may, instead (or also), have been leather or padded linen. This cut-down cap appears on a fragment of relief found at Sakkara, where a stack of six New Kingdom helmets sits next to six shields. Another fragment from the same site provides a clue as to the material that these helmets were made from; on it, an official weighs three cap-style helmets on a balance, something difficult to explain unless they were made of bronze. Like all metals, bronze had intrinsic value, and its net worth could be assessed simply by placing it on a scale. It is hard to reconcile the image on the Sakkara fragment if the cap helmets were made simply of leather or padded linen.

It is clear, however, that helmets (of bronze or any other material) were not standard issue and relatively few New Kingdom soldiers are shown wearing them. The most common head-covering of the Nineteenth Dynasty was the striped head-cloth, an item more of status and prestige than protection.

Egyptian Body Armour

Most reliefs portray the Egyptian soldier without armour, although there are a number of depictions of body armour dated to the Old and Middle Kingdom. This armour seems to have been in the form of white cloth bands that were worn over both shoulders and that crossed the chest——a form of protection that echoed the *tutittu* worn by Sumerian troops in Mesopotamia. Although these heavy bands might have been made of leather, the white colouring on the wall paintings suggests that they were instead made up of layers of linen glued together. This type of defence served the heavy infantry hoplites of Greece well during the classical period, proving to be a lighter, cheaper, and more common form of body armour than the famous bronze breastplate. Its strength came from the many layers of linen, made stiff by the hide glue used to bind them together. *Tutittu* and its Egyptian equivalent (*qenyeh*) may have been manufactured in exactly this way. Unit commanders sometimes benefitted from the additional protection of a copper or bronze disc inserted beneath the centre of the textile banding, an example of this enhanced armour is depicted on the walls of a tomb at El Berseh.

While we cannot be certain that these bands of cloth do indeed represent body armour, battle reliefs from the New Kingdom certainly do show foot soldiers clad in some form of banded textile armour. New Kingdom styles differ markedly from those of earlier ages, replacing the cross-banding with horizontal bands of leather or stiffened linen. The effect is remarkably similar to that of the classic Roman legionary with his shirt of *lorica segmentata*, an arrangement of iron hoops that circled his chest and that were fastened together with leather straps and bronze buckles. The bands of armour worn by Ramses the Great's soldiers were not metal, however, and in the reliefs to which paint still adheres, the armour is coloured white, buff, or brown, suggesting linen, leather, or some other soft and flexible material.

Styles vary, some soldiers are shown with textile bands wrapped around the chest all the way down to the waist and kilt, others have left a gap, with the midriff visible, with the linen bands wrapped around the upper chest only. Some of the soldiers have one band looping over one shoulder, leaving the opposite arm and shoulder unprotected. Such variation suggests that a single protective garment was not issued to the troops in the New Kingdom, but that various types were available or perhaps that troops themselves improvised various styles of linen body armour. Based on the surviving depictions of storerooms full of helmets and craftsmen hard at work producing shields for the pharaoh's army, it is, however, more likely that armour was issued by the state—although it did not always conform to a standard design.

Armour of the Sea Peoples

The arrival of those enigmatic foreigners, the Sea Peoples, introduced wholly new types of armour into the Near East and the first of the European mercenaries to arrive were the *Shardana*. Almost eighty years prior to the Sea Peoples invasions that occurred around 1,200 BC, groups of *Shardana* were already fighting for pharaoh as an elite unit of infantrymen. Their helmets are shallow bronze caps that sport a pair of short horns mounted either side of a disc (or sphere) that sits between them. This decorative 'sun disc' was an Egyptian affectation—when *Shardana* appear as part of the Sea Peoples' attack on the Nile Delta in 1,187 BC, their helmets lack the sun disc element, yet retain the horns.

The armour worn by Ramses the Great's *Shardana* guardsmen (as depicted on the Kadesh reliefs at Abu Simbel) was of a unique style, not seen in the Near East before this time; it took the form of a jerkin of stiff panels or plates fastened to a flexible backing with prominent rivets. Four strips curved around the chest, and these were held in position by two broad shoulder straps of similar construction. Additional panels formed a kilt that included cut-outs on each thigh, which perhaps eased movement of the warrior's legs. Like scale coats, this inflexible laminar armour was fastened on the left (shielded) side. Some reliefs at Abu

Two *Shardana* warriors; these are allies of Egypt as the sun discs atop their helmets show. The (presumably metal) discs on their shields are an interesting detail, but it is the unusual laminar style armour that makes this carving unique. The long swords have been emphasised in this relief.

Simbel show the armour fastening on the right-hand side, but this occurs only when Shardana are facing each other in a symmetrical, mirror-image composition. Laminar armour (armour that is made up of rows or bands of solid plates) is known from other cultures around the world. The Roman legions made iron laminar armour famous, while the native tribes of Alaska and Siberia, such as the Aleut and Chugach people, made their laminar from bone, baleen, or wood

The armour was certainly rigid, but whether the material used in its construction was horn, bronze, or wood, we do not know. Bronze is most likely, particularly when one considers the status of the *Shardana* guardsmen as well as the fact that a number of elite native Egyptian units are also shown wearing this exotic cuirass. Not only the *Shardana*, but some Egyptian archers (perhaps dismounted chariot warriors), some of the chariotry, and the native royal guards also wear this laminar coat. The armour type must have carried with it a certain cachet, but it is not seen again among the Egyptian army and may have been uniquely associated with the combat techniques of the European *Shardana* who fought with long rapiers and round shields—they were close-range swordsmen, just like the Roman legionaries, and they must have needed this heavy protection in order to survive the onslaught of fierce, face-to-face, and hand-to-hand fighting.

When we meet the *Shardana* again, it is as aggressors within the coalition of Sea Peoples that made repeated attacks on the Egyptian Delta in the decades either side of 1,200 BC. These new *Shardana* still retain the bronze cap with its distinctive horns, they carry the same round shields, and still fight with swords, however, their style of armour has changed. Allies of the *Shardana*, the *Peleset*, *Tjekker* and *Denyen*, are identified by their distinctive headdresses of animal hair; they also wear this new style of armour—it was an advanced form of bronze segmented body armour with all the hallmarks of Mycenaean (Bronze Age Greek) technology.

This advanced bronze armour featured rounded shoulder plates, each with a central stud. Around the torso wrapped half a dozen metal bands, creating a distinctive V-shape (sometimes an inverted 'V' depending on the wearer's tribe) across the abdomen. Unlike the scale coat, as well as the earlier *Shardana* cuirass, this protection ended at the waist, which points to the use of bronze in its construction rather than leather. Both the rounded shoulder pieces and overlapping body plates suggest a close affinity with the famous Dendra panoply, now on display in Nafplion museum in Greece and dated to around 1,400 BC. The plethora of horned helmets appearing in Mycenaean frescoes between 1,300 BC and 1,100 BC also suggest some link between the *Shardana* and the Mycenaean warriors of Bronze Age Greece. Robert Drews explained the rise of the armour-clad, mercenary swordsman as a new phenomenon, a

A ship of the Sea Peoples, part of the attack on the Nile Delta during the reign of Ramses III. This vessel is not depicted with oars and both its prow and stern are very high. The warriors are all *Shardana*, hostile to Egypt, and they wear a new form of bronze armour reminiscent of the Dendra panoply found in Bronze Age Greece.

tribal counter to the expensive chariot-using armies of the Near Eastern palace kingdoms. Drews' persuasive hypothesis suggests that it was these bands of close-combat, armoured swordsmen that destroyed many of the palace civilisations and brought a chaotic and violent end to the Bronze Age and to Egyptian supremacy in the ancient world.

Aftermath

Following a battle or a skirmish, it was customary for troops to reward themselves with any booty they found on the battlefield. This was seen by commanders as a just reward for the common soldier in payment for his hard work, rough treatment, and courage in the face of mutilation or death. There were rules, however; soldiers in the Egyptian army were able to take their pick of common objects, but anything of value had to be handed in to the scribes for assessment and accounting. Some of this treasure would then be used by pharaoh and his staff to reward and remunerate the troops thought to be most deserving. Ahmose-Pen-Nekhbet, an officer fighting for Tuthmosis II in Syria, was rewarded for his loyalty with gold—two gold bracelets, four gold necklaces, one armlet, two golden axes, and six 'flies'. This last reward was an official one, small flies cast in solid gold that spoke of the warrior's bravery and tenacity in war. We may assume that these chariot warriors, company commanders, and other officers passed some this considerable wealth down to the men in the lower ranks.

Although the looting of bodies and supply wagons on the battlefield was supposed to occur once the battle was over, it seems that the troops doing the fighting and the commander of the army often had different ideas about what constituted 'over'. Pharaoh Tuthmosis III's attempt to capture the city of Megiddo was scotched when some of his troops failed to pursue the fleeing Canaanites and instead looted the corpses of the dead. 'Then were captured their horses, their chariots of gold and silver were made spoil; their champions lay stretched out like fishes on the ground'—this allusion to fishes may reflect bronze 'fish-scale' armour of the dead *maryannu* chariot warriors. Pharaoh, in the Annals, rebukes his men and blames the loss of the city on their greed.

There was certainly a great deal to lose, for when the city did eventually fall to a prolonged siege later that year, the spoil included all of the fabulous wealth of both the king of Megiddo and also the chief of Kadesh, who had also been trapped within the walls. There were definitely sound strategic reasons for launching military campaigns into Syria, and for capturing cities, but the real prize was always spoil. Megiddo, for example, rendered the following prizes:

> 340 living prisoners; 83 hands; 2,041 mares; 191 foals; 6 stallions...; a chariot wrought with gold belonging to the chief of Megiddo; 892 chariots

> of the wretched army...; a beautiful suit of bronze armour belonging to the king of Kadesh; a beautiful suit of bronze armour belonging to the chief of Megiddo; 200 suits of armour belonging to his wretched army; 502 bows; 7 poles of wood... 1,929 large cattle, 2,000 small cattle; 20,500 white small cattle (perhaps sheep).
>
> The Annals

This list is packed with military equipment, something New Kingdom Egypt valued over all things. Tributes from Canaan often came in the form of chariots, composite bows, bronze helmets, and coats of scale armour. These things Egypt needed in great quantities, and she had determined that it was easier to demand them from her vassal states rather than call for silver and pay its workers to imitate them. Less well-endowed cities were forced to hand over whatever they had, however mundane. In the aftermath of the sack of Megiddo, the neighbouring towns were plundered by Tuthmosis, and brought him all manner of spoil. He took 1,796 male and female slaves (with their children), flat dishes, vases, knives, the chairs and footstools of the nobility, a wooden staff, bronze vessels, and statues made of wood and covered in gold. Certainly there were true treasures within that haul, including gold rings, silver statues, and even a sceptre encrusted with jewels. As if to hammer home the prosaic nature of much of the plunder, the plain of Megiddo was harvested and its grain carried off as booty. It yielded, to the scribes who counted it, 208,200 fourfold *heket* of grain, 'besides that which was cut as forage by the army'.

As Tuthmosis III in the Annals made clear, there were rules that soldiers had to follow, and soldiers could be punished for breaking them. On one occasion, soldiers stole leather hides from local people that were destined for the taxmen. When their crimes were discovered, the men responsible were given 100 lashes and had 'five wounds' opened up on their bodies. The harsh discipline of the army forced some to flee and these deserters were hunted down by military scouts using tracker dogs. If they could not be found, then the deserter's family could instead be imprisoned, serving as a deterrent for other recruits also contemplating desertion.

7

Hand-to-Hand Weapons

Menna, my shield-bearer, knew that a legion of chariots surrounded me.
He became weak—his heart was faint. Terror was in his limbs.

Kadesh relief, Temple of Amun at Karnak

Use of the Spear

Spearmen, armed with both a shield (*ikem*) and a spear (*dja*), formed the core of most ancient armies. The spear required a relatively small amount of metal in its construction, equivalent to that of a dagger, which meant that the weapon was cheap to make and therefore a suitable weapon for large numbers of troops.

Many Egyptian reliefs from the new Kingdom period illustrate units of spearmen, and these reliefs have antecedents in the Middle and Old Kingdoms. For example, Tutankhamun's royal guards are shown on the lid of a chest discovered within his tomb—they follow behind their master as he shoots arrows from a chariot. In one register, six infantrymen strike out and five of them carry spears as well as a sidearm, either an axe, a club, or both. Three of these men also carry shields. This is a mixed unit, with a variety of hand-weapons and a smattering of shields—one of the guards even carries a bow along with his spear. Perhaps a more regular phalanx of Egyptian spearmen is depicted on reliefs from Queen Hatshepsut's Temple at Deir el-Bahri. Eight soldiers march in close order and carry both shield and spear in their left hand. The men at the head and the tail of the file are shown with axes in their right hands, although it is unclear whether the rest of the phalanx carry this sidearm behind their shields. An archer walks ahead of the unit with his bow tucked away in its leather case; this bow replaces his shield, although he still carried a spear and an axe. Similar units of spearmen are found on reliefs from across New Kingdom Egypt, suggesting that this troop type dominated the ranks of the infantry division. A junior officer often follows or leads the unit, and his authority and role as military disciplinarian is typically marked by the stick he carries, reminiscent of the Roman centurion's *vitus* or olive-wood swagger stick.

Another depiction of spearmen appears on the grand battle relief of Medinet Habu, portraying Ramses III's victory over an invading Libyan army. Egyptian chariots are charging into the fray, while a small unit of close-order spearmen march ahead of them, in support of allied Sea Peoples who are fighting hand-to-hand with the Libyans. While they march boldly forward, these Egyptian spearmen carry a spear over one shoulder and either an axe or curved sword (*khopesh*); all have a shield strapped onto their spear arm. It is clear from the way in which the artist has rendered the individual figures that they are intended to be part of a close-order, highly regimented fighting unit.

The unwieldy nature of the spear when used offensively by a soldier on the battlefield meant that attacks could only be met from the front. To counter this disadvantage, spearmen fought in closely packed formations and defended themselves with hand-held shields. This 'strength in numbers' tactic strengthened the flanks of the troops within that unit, providing a measure of security as they moved forward to engage an enemy force.

Both shield and spear complimented one another—the spear was thrust forward into the target, past the shield, yet allowed the attacker to remain behind that shield. Other weapons, like the axe and sword, forced the attacker to reach forward, exposing his right arm and shoulder to attacks from his opponent. It was the relative length of the wooden spear shaft that allowed the infantryman to fight from behind his shield in this manner. Prime target areas would have been the face and upper chest, the groin, thighs, and legs—and all would have been in reach of the spear.

Paintings and reliefs help us understand how the Egyptians wielded the spear in battle (or at least what the sculptors and painters understood of contemporary combat manoeuvres). The typical attack pose shows the infantryman with shield held forward away from his body and the spear held high ready for an overarm thrust. Modern studies have indicated that a spear strike in this manner has a speed of 17 metres per second and an impact energy of around 9.7 metre-kilogrammes, comparable to the blow from a wide-bladed cutting axe.

Ancient cavalry, and by extension chariot horses, found a wall of spears and shields very intimidating and infantry units were wary of advancing on a formation of spearmen unless they had long spears themselves with which to reach their foes. That was the great advantage of the spear over other weapons: it had great defensive value and, if used in conjunction with others, was able to keep an attacker well beyond arm's length. Spears could be used overarm to stab down onto a foe, over his shield; however, to do this, the spear must be held near to the mid-point and was greatly foreshortened. In addition to losing the great advantage of the spear—its length—attacking overarm presented a spearman's right arm, armpit, and right chest to the attacker. Better was the underarm spear thrust. The spear was held closer to the butt, which tucked under the forearm. Held like this, the spear was stabbed powerfully forward into an enemy without exposing oneself to attack. It also allowed better control of the spear shaft for raking aside an enemy spear or for parrying the spear thrust of a foe.

Reconstructions of spear and shield-fighting methods have shown that the spear is effective when used in a dense formation, but is ungainly and disadvantaged when used in open skirmishing warfare. Of course, any modern reconstruction cannot do justice to the power and lethality of these weapons. Any form of weapon re-enactment is bound by strict safety rules, although it is clear that the most vulnerable targets open to a spear-wielding legionary are the face and shins of an enemy warrior—exactly those areas of the body strictly off-limits as target areas in modern battle re-enactments. The author participated in an experiment to recreate two battle lines coming into contact. Prior to the shield walls slamming together, the (blunted) spear-points slid off of the shield boards and everyone involved had to keep their heads down to avoid getting a spear point in the face. One participant was unlucky enough to receive a very minor cut to the cheek. Spear points also slid down towards the shins and feet, though with much less danger of serious injury.

Spear Design

New Kingdom spears were cast in bronze and socketed—that is, the spearhead included a socket or hollow at its base into which the wooden spear shaft (*mahut*) was rammed. This was a technological innovation that arrived with the Hyksos and which, like the chariot and the composite bow, had been adopted enthusiastically by the Egyptian army. Prior to the socketed spear, the native Egyptian spearhead had ended in a sharp spike (or tang) that was rammed into the end of a wooden spear shaft. The problem with this Old Kingdom method of fixing was that every thrust against an opponent's shield or body drove the head (and the tang) deeper into the shaft, splitting the wooden apart. Each thrust of the new socketed spear, however, simply forced the bronze head more tightly onto the wooden shaft. This did not make the spear indestructible, however; Roman accounts mention socketed spears snapping in combat, and Egyptian spears would have fared no better.

> In this scene of total confusion the infantry, worn out by toil and danger, had no strength or sense left to form a plan. Most had their spears shattered in the constant collisions, so they made do with their drawn swords...
>
> Ammianus Marcellinus 31.13

No doubt this tendency of spears to break during the furious hand-to-hand exchanges of combat required spearmen to carry a sidearm, such as a club, axe, dagger, or *khopesh*.

Many of the beautiful leaf-shaped spearheads that have been recovered from burials were inscribed. It is clear that the blades were cast with a pronounced mid-rib running vertically down the centre of the blade, which provided strength and rigidity, preventing the blade from bending on impact with either a shield or the bone within an impaled victim. The lack of a sharply defined tip on most Egyptian spearheads, and the rounded, leaf-like nature of the blades' shape suggest that this weapon realised its greatest killing potential against unarmoured opponents. They were designed specifically to open up a wound that was as long as possible in order to maximise shock and blood loss.

Spears are commonly depicted under 2 metres in length, which classifies them as short spears, and as such, they would have been easily thrown at an opponent in the manner of an *ad hoc* javelin. However, there are no illustrations of the short spear being used by Egyptian forces in this way since dedicated javelins seem to have always been on hand to fulfil the requirements of ranged combat. One scene on Tutankhamun's painted box graphically illustrates the death of enemy charioteers at the hands of Egyptian spearmen. These troops are wielding extremely short stabbing spears that are around a metre in length, with both hands fiercely plunging them into the bodies of the enemy. The heads of these stabbing spears make up half or more of this length, as a 60-cm-long example in the Ashmolean Museum in Oxford confirms. This example was inscribed with the name Kamose, which places it firmly within the Eighteenth Dynasty. Such short, long-bladed weapons resemble the deadly *falx* that were used with such effectiveness against Emperor Trajan's Roman legions in Dacia. Such an unusual New Kingdom weapon (nowhere else recorded) may well have developed from the use of javelins by the infantrymen in close-in, hand-to-hand fighting.

Javelins

While the dedicated throwing spear or javelin, common throughout the ancient Near East, was commonly derived from the infantryman's regular stabbing spear, the weapon had a unique design all of its own in Egypt. The javelins (*nesyut*) of the New Kingdom were short, around a metre in length, enabling a soldier to carry several within a quiver that he carried over his shoulder. Most are depicted with diamond-shaped heads, and in some scenes the javelins are fletched to provide stability as it travels through the air—similar to arrows. Indeed, where arrows are shown impaling the bodies of Egypt's enemies, it is unclear whether they are actually javelins or arrows that have been shot from a bow. Furthermore, despite the modern view of the javelin as a one-shot, disposable missile, the Egyptian javelin was typically fitted with a sturdy, reinforced grip made of wood or metal. The grip allowed a firm hold on the weapon and also served as a counterbalance to the metal blade. Here we see the javelin as a dual-purpose weapon, used primarily for close-combat thrusting in combination with a shield, but it was a weapon that could be effectively thrown.

This added further to the Egyptian army's already formidable missile capability derived from its deployment of large numbers of archers.

Reinforcing this view of the Egyptian javelin as a tool for close-in killing as well as ranged combat, it should be noted that there are probably more illustrations of javelins being used in hand-to-hand fighting than there are javelins in flight. The weapon is typically shown being used aggressively by infantrymen to despatch enemy soldiers. However, the javelin as missile weapon can be seen clearly on the battle reliefs of Medinet Habu, where the Egyptian navy of Ramses III drives off an invading fleet of Sea Peoples. Marines on the deck of pharaoh's warships are armed either with composite bows or with shield and javelin. Each javelin looks to be about a metre in length and ends in what appears to be arrow-like fletchings. With shield held out, away from the body, the marines grasp the javelin close to the end of the shaft, just ahead of the fletchings. Many Sea Peoples in the scene have been pierced by arrows or javelins and fallen from their ships, although, as already noted, it is almost impossible to differentiate between the two types of missile.

Chariots served as mobile weapons platforms within the Egyptian army, and they are frequently illustrated with a small arsenal of weapons on board. Typically, a quiver full of arrows and a club are mounted on one side of the chariot cab, while a separate quiver that contains a number of javelins is fixed to the other. Only the grips are visible, but those mounted on the chariot of Ramses II (that adorns part of the Kadesh relief in the Ramesseum) provide fascinating detail. The grips of the royal javelins flare out at the butt, presumably to prevent them slipping from one's grasp during close combat. There are no fletchings in evidence on these javelins. They are decorated, either painted or inlaid, and a pommel or spherical terminal at the end of the grip is further decorated with a couple of fringed tassels.

Behind the Shield

Contrary to the battle scenes in most Hollywood and TV movies, the ancient soldier fought with a wooden shield for defence. For a relatively low cost, foot soldiers were given the ability to block incoming attacks for as long as they were able. No shield guaranteed safety on the battlefield, but it provided the defence that was needed in order to make an attack of one's own. With the development of the infantry phalanx, shields could be brought together to form a wall from behind which the Egyptian troops could mount an attack. Meanwhile, their opponents were doing the same.

Shields (*ikem*) of the Old Kingdom included large 'body shields' that suggest combat in a pre-phalanx age, but by the Middle Kingdom, as the painted wooden models from the tomb of Meseheti at Asyut show, shields were becoming smaller and more regular in shape. Eighteenth Dynasty shields were between 1 metre

Remains of the temple of Montuhotep II at Deir el-Bahri. (*Author's Collection*)

Nubian prisoners of war, arms bound behind their backs. A relief from the temple of Amun at Thebes. (*Author's Collection*)

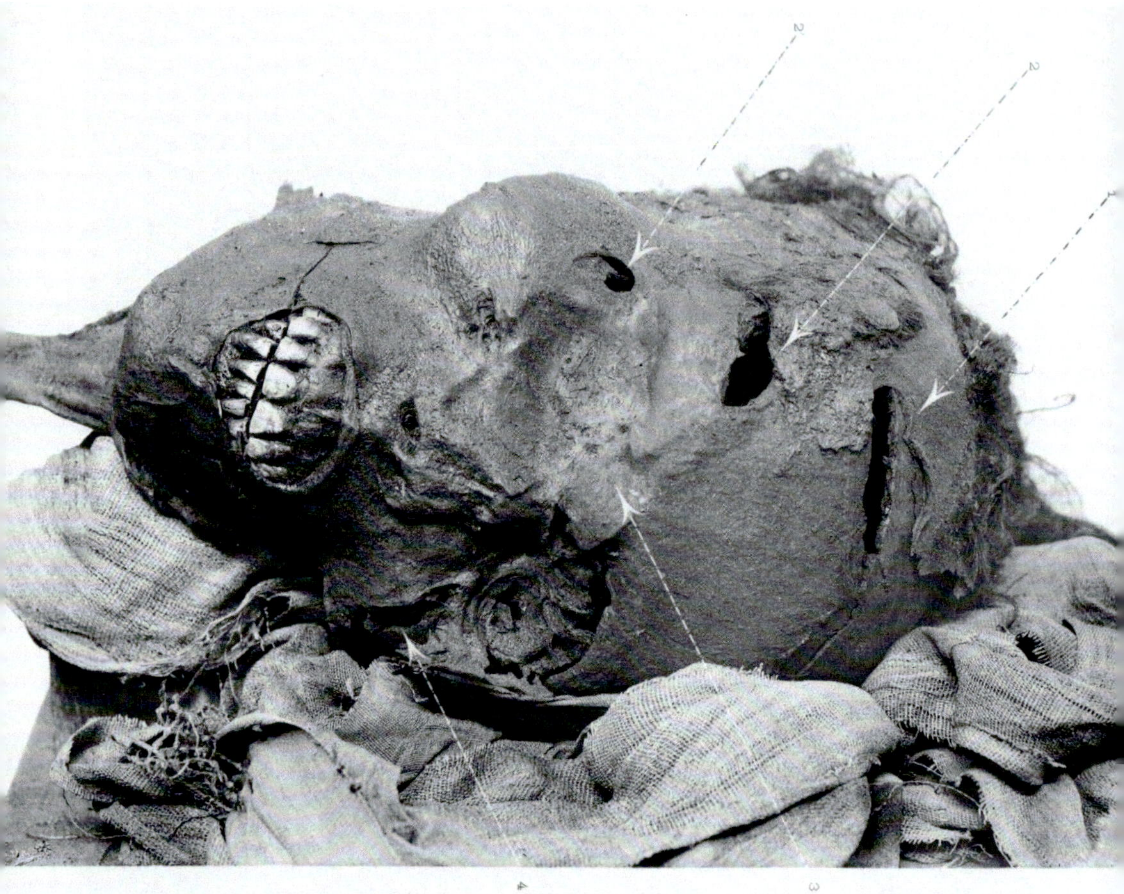

The extraordinary mummy of Pharaoh Seqenenre Tao, with obvious head wounds. This pharaoh probably died in battle attempting to wrestle Egypt from the foreign Hyksos. (*G. Elliot Smith, Public domain via Wikimedia Commons*)

Semitic Bedouin—or *hikau khasut*—with spears, a throwstick, composite bow, and waterskin, from the Middle Kingdom tomb of Khnumhotep II at Beni Hasan. (*Carl Richard Lepsius, public domain via Wikimedia Commons*)

The Hittite peace treaty with Egypt, recorded by Hittite scribes in Akkadian cuneiform. Now in the Istanbul Archaeology Museum. (*Monsieurdl via Wikimedia Commons*)

Above: Ramses II's spectacular temple at Abu Simbel. The reliefs within its rock-cut corridors recount the pharaoh's battle against the Hittites at Kadesh. (*Author's Collection*)

Below: Nubian prisoners being threatened with a beating by Egyptian soldiers. A military scribe records the selection of one of the Nubians for the court of Tutankhamun. From the tomb of Horemheb. (*Sailko, CC BY-SA 3.0 via Wikimedia Commons*)

Above: Soldiers during the reign of Horemheb carry a tree trunk. They wear helmets and leather 'naval' webbing over their linen kilts. Note how flexible the triangle of fabric is that hangs between their legs. (*Sailko, CC BY-SA 3.0 via Wikimedia Commons*)

Below: A group of soldiers from the Amarna period armed with clubs; they venerate either the pharaoh or their own general.
(*Brooklyn Museum, Charles Edwin Wilbour Fund, 32.103. Creative Commons*)

Replica of a royal shield at the Tutankhamun exhibit in Berlin, 2013. The backing leather is missing. (*Thomas Quine, Creative Commons Attribution*)

Fragment of a relief that shows an Egyptian spearman on a siege ladder. He clutches a spear in his left hand, while his straight-sided shield is looped over his shoulder on a sling. (*Brooklyn Museum, Charles Edwin Wilbour Fund, 77.130. Creative Commons*)

The famous Florence chariot, the earliest extant chariot from ancient Egypt. Dated to the Eighteenth Dynasty, the chariot now resides in the *Museo Archeologico Nazionale* in Florence, Italy. (*Khruner via Wikimedia Commons*)

A chariot and its team of horses, from the Amarna period. One horse looks at the viewer, something unknown in ancient Egyptian art.
(*Brooklyn Museum, Gift of New Hermes Foundation, 60.28. Creative Commons*)

Replica of the golden chariot at the Tutankhamun exhibit in Berlin, 2013. Only pharaoh's chariot featured the Horus statue topped by the sun disc. The wide wheel base is well-displayed here. (*Claude Valette, Creative Commons Attribution*)

A scimitar sword (*khopesh*) from the reign of Ramses II. Note the cast bronze grip. Earlier *khopesh* had much shorter, curved sections to the blade.
(*Guillaume Blanchard via WikiCommons*)

A relief of infantrymen from the temple of Luxor. They carry curved sickle swords (*khopesh*) and the straight-sided shields of the Nineteenth Dynasty (here they are tipped forward). (*Author's Collection*)

A New Kingdom openwork axe blade, beautifully cast in bronze. It depicts a graceful ibex lowering its head to eat. (*Charles Edwin Wilbour Fund, 66.171.1. Creative Commons*)

This tanged axe has been detached from its haft. It shows the way in which the back of the blade sat in a groove within the wood and how leather thongs bound the slightly splayed upper and lower edges of the blade to the haft. (*Author's Collection*)

A copper axe blade inscribed with the titulary of Pharaoh Ahmose I. This pharaoh successfully threw out the Hyksos from Egypt and established the New Kingdom. (*Iry-Hor via Wikimedia Commons*)

Battle-axes with unclear origins. Note the wide, splayed cutting edge of the central axe head, perfect for striking unarmoured targets. These blades undoubtedly date from the Old or Middle Kingdom. (*Khruner via Wikimedia Commons*)

Bronze dagger—complete with wooden haft—that bears the cartouche of Pharaoh Thutmose IV, Eighteenth Dynasty. (*Khruner via Wikimedia Commons*)

Shardana warriors in the service of Ramses III. Their round shields, rapier-like swords, and helmets sporting horns and a sun-disc are distinctive. Enemy *Shardana* looked almost identical, but lacked the sun-disc motif. (*By Olaf Tausch via Wikimedia Commons*)

Above: A beautifully decorated royal throwstick made of ivory at the Tutankhamun exhibit in Berlin, 2013. (*Thomas Quine, Creative Commons Attribution*)

Right: Composite bows and decorated bow case at the Tutankhamun exhibit in Berlin, 2013. This royal example terminates in a golden lion head. (*Thomas Quine, Creative Commons Attribution*)

Rear face of the two replica shields. The example on the left is fitted with a shoulder strap.

Opposite above: Replica Egyptian carpentry tools. *From left to right*: bow drill, awl, chisel and polishing stone, hand saw, and malachite (copper ore). Malachite was mined in Sinai for the production of bronze. A lucky scarab sits beside the awl. (*Author's Collection*)

Opposite below: Two replica shields constructed by the author using his Egyptian carpentry tools. The smaller shield is an Eighteenth Dynasty design, while its companion resembles those carried by soldiers of Ramses II at Kadesh. (*Author's Collection*)

Spear and shield held together, as depicted in the reliefs of soldiers depicted at Deir el-Bahri.

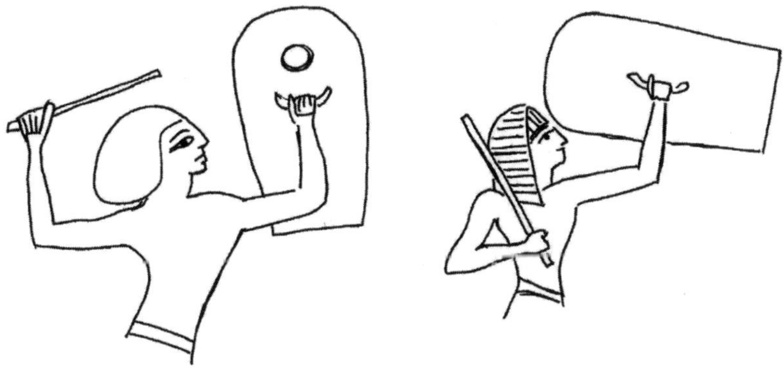

Shields are generally well-illustrated in battle reliefs; here, the grips vary in orientation, although the majority of Egyptian depictions favour the vertical-style grip.

and 75 cm in height and around 50 cm wide; they were roughly rectangular in shape, with a curved upper edge and tapering sides. In some depictions, a central panel or band bore the name of the pharaoh and, possibly, the name of the unit the solder was a part of. Some of the shields found with Tutankhamun were of this design and constructed from three vertical panels of light wood that had been covered with a facing of cheetah or antelope hide. Wooden edging had also been added to strengthen the shield and a bronze panel was nailed to the centre of each shield-board in order to provide some protection for the hand of the shield user. On the painted lid of Tutankhamun's wooden chest, the shields carried by his soldiers display all of these qualities, along with the addition of a decorative painted border around their edge. Common soldiers would have made do with a covering of something less exotic, usually cow skin, either glued onto the shield-board or simply painted on with black and tan paint—in imitation of the real thing.

By the Nineteenth Dynasty, shields had become more rectangular, although they retained the curved upper edge. The more professional and well-trained infantrymen of Ramses I and his successors were now able to fight in compact units, shield-to-shield, and they required a uniform design of shield that would allow them to present an unbroken shield wall to their enemies. There is no reason to doubt that shields were still constructed from three thin planks of wood; however, the face of the shield was now gessoed and then painted a plain colour, such as red or blue. Where the reliefs show detail, the facing is often bordered by thin bands of colour. The upper faces of Nineteenth and Twentieth Dynasties shields were usually reinforced with a bronze disc that was flanked by two sacred cobras, an allusion to another of the royal emblems: the *uraeus*. Symbolising the protective goddess Wadjet, the *uraeus* was worn only by the gods Horus and Set and, of course, on the crown of the pharaoh.

A pair of Egyptian infantrymen of the Nineteenth Dynasty with distinctive striped head-cloths, short spears, curved shields that are perhaps carried on straps, and hand weapons (a *khopesh* and short sword).

When a defender brought the shield up to protect his face, the bronze disc will have provided extra protection from an enemy axe, spear, or sword. As a point of interest, Egyptian troops dressed in the manner of Sea Peoples carried these rectangular shields into battle, but the sun and cobra design on the face of each had been replaced by what appears to be a wheel.

Shield grips on the rear of the board were carved from wood and mounted centrally. Unlike Roman shield grips, which ran horizontally, the Egyptian grips ran vertically, which meant the soldier held the shield much like a spear. Leather or cord straps are often shown attached to the backs of shields, probably tied or threaded through the handgrip. These straps allowed soldiers to carry a shield on their back during a long march or when involved in physical activity like undermining the walls of an enemy city or climbing a siege ladder. A siege scene dated from the reign of Ramses II, at the Karnak temple, shows infantrymen with shields strapped to their backs doing both of these, as well as one trooper with his hands busy, grasping the hair of a Canaanite victim with one and hacking at his throat with another.

Shields were stored in armouries established at temples and garrisons across Egypt, and certain officials were tasked with their manufacture and supply. Remarkably, a relief depicting activity within a shield workshop

Jumping from the lion-headed prow of an Egyptian ship, these marines wield clubs and carry rounded shields. Note that the soldier on the left wears a Syrian-style reinforced kilt, a fashion trend adopted from foreign mercenaries employed by the Egyptian army.

survives from the tomb of Mahu, dating from the Amarna period. It depicts a workman stretching a cowhide over a wooden former that will be used as the facing for a shield.

Auxiliary troops like the Libyans, Nubians, and the *Shardana* brought with them distinctive shield designs of their own. Those of the *Shardana* hint at a new style of hand-to-hand combat, since the combination of round shield and long bronze sword was suited more to one-on-one fighting rather than a massed phalanx waging war from behind a shield wall. These round shields seem to have been faced with leather and then covered with a number of metal discs. When Ramses III's fleet countered an attack by the warships of the Sea Peoples in 1,187 BC, the Egyptian marines adopted the bronze breastplates of the very people they were fighting, yet they continued to fight with their own rectangular shields and did not adopt the Sea Peoples' panoply wholesale. However, an earlier encounter between Sea Peoples and Egyptian chariots in 1,184 BC suggests that the round shield of the seaborne mercenaries did find a role within pharaoh's army. A mixed wagon train of Sea Peoples refugees and warriors is shown at Medinet Habu under fierce attack from Egyptian soldiers and allied *Shardana* mercenaries. Beneath a large-scale relief of Ramses III unleashing arrows from his chariot, a squadron of his chariots plunges into the fray, each

Above left: An unusual depiction of a curved shield. This may not be representative as many other representations clearly show the Egyptian shield to be flat.

Above right: In the Nineteenth and Twentieth Dynasties, only the Sea Peoples and foreign mercenaries carried round shields. Here, however, in a detail from Ramses III's temple at Medinet Habu, Egyptian chariot crews are depicted with these round shields as their vehicles mow down arrow-pierced *Peleset*.

vehicle carrying a driver who is protecting his warrior with a round shield. Shields of this shape do not appear in Egyptian iconography before this time.

Libyans seem to have fought without the protection of shields, while the Nubian tribesmen carried simple oval shields, each formed from a light-weight wooden frame covered with a stretched animal hide. Similar shield designs remained popular amongst East African tribes for thousands of years. A Zulu shield, brought back to England as a trophy by a British soldier from the 1879 Battle of Isandlwana, was sold at auction in 2014. Of a similar size to those depicted on the Nubian reliefs, the Zulu shield was made of dried cowhide stretched over a wooden framework.

Use of the Axe

> King Okhepernere (Tuthmosis II), triumphant, gave to me of gold: three bracelets, six necklaces, three armlets ... a silver axe.
>
> Biography of Ahmose-Pen-Nekhbet

Along with the spear, the hand-axe or hatchet (*ikhu*) is the weapon most commonly carried by Egyptian soldiers in reliefs and wall paintings. It was an ancient weapon, employed by all of the Near Eastern civilisations, but again—as with the bow and the chariot—Egyptian military technology lagged significantly behind that of neighbouring kingdoms. The New Kingdom infantrymen were carrying a type of axe on to the battlefield that had been superseded by a more advanced form centuries earlier. Egyptian conservatism, the reliance on techniques and technologies that were proven to work against the traditional foes of Egypt, won out over military advancement and evolution.

In several depictions of infantry units, spearmen hold both spear and shield in their left hand, with a secondary weapon (often an axe) clutched in their right. Reliefs from Queen Hatshepsut's mortuary temple at Deir el-Bahri show some of these soldiers holding their axes in this way. Whereas most cultures (including the Hittites) depict the axe held with blade facing forward, the Egyptian artists almost universally include a tiny detail—men carrying their axe on the march or on parade grip the wooden haft just below the bronze axe-head, while the head itself is always shown reversed, pointing towards the owner. This jars the modern viewer, it does not seem quite right, but the detail probably records an actual element of Egyptian infantry drill. Modern soldiers in the West may flinch in a similar manner when they see guerrilla troops in TV news broadcasts that are carrying their assault rifles over their shoulders, upside down, gripping the barrel with their hand while the butt of the rifle lays across their shoulder.

From the Middle Kingdom temple of Montuhotep II, at Deir el-Bahri, comes a fragmentary relief that depicts an Egyptian archer with an axe tucked into his belt. This must have proven a very effective and practical method of carrying the hand-axe. In the relief, the soldier clutches both a bow and a number of arrows in his right hand, but we cannot see what he carries in his left. Other evidence supports this practice, with axes being shown tucked into belts at the back of the kilt or underneath the strap-like bands of armour (*qenyeh*) that some infantryman wore. A number of wooden axe hafts discovered by archaeologists have been pierced by a hole bored through them near the end of the haft. Obviously, this suggests the use of a leather thong, either to secure the axe to the owner's wrist for security in hand-to-hand combat or to allow the axe to be hung easily from kit, over the shoulder, or from a carrying pole (the use of kit poles used to carry military equipment is mentioned in Chapter 6)—perhaps while on the march.

The persistence of the axe within the Egyptian army can perhaps be explained by its other use—as a tool. Art provides us with a number of examples of soldiers who use their military axes for another purpose, such as cutting down trees during siege operations in order to build siege equipment. Others involved in siege operations use the axe to undermine city walls. The siege of a Canaanite city is depicted in a relief at Ramses III's temple at Medinet Habu, although scholars have argued whether this pharaoh ever besieged a Palestinian city. The relief shows troops under the shadow of the walls hacking at the city foundations with their axes, while a number of their comrades fell trees in the surrounding countryside. As already noted, all of these axe-men have strapped their shields on to their backs in order to allow them to wield their axes with two hands. Representations of the weapon are also found in other contexts—a number of axes are shown as items of tribute within the tombs of notables such as Antef and Rekhmire. Within the tombs of Menkheperrasonb and Ipuimre, however, axes are instead shown during the manufacturing process. In the New Kingdom tomb of Ineni, axes are carried by a number of soldiers or guards as part of a procession; one man waves his axe threateningly in the air to cow a group of female prisoners.

Axe Design

The axe originally developed in other areas of the Near East as an improvement on the oldest of hand weapons—the club or mace. The axe retained the weight and kinetic force of the mace, but added the additional murderous refinement of a cutting edge to open up human bodies and spill their blood. Axe design changed, even in Egypt, to overcome the defensive measures being adopted by soldiers on the battlefield who wished to protect themselves from the damage wrought by the bronze war axe.

A universal problem encountered by all ancient axe-using cultures was the mechanism by which the blade was attached to the wooden haft. The weaker this fastening, the less force could be applied during a strike, thus lessening the killing impact of the weapon. More elaborate attachment methods that utilised the shape of the bronze head itself required advancements in bronze casting; the simple flat axes employed by the New Kingdom infantry units were instead reliant on weak wooden and leather fastenings. This was the difference between tanged and socketed axes. The tanged axe was simply a flat piece of axe-shaped bronze that was sharpened at the business end; the opposite end was slotted into a groove cut down one side of the wooden haft. Jammed into this slot, glued and bound with rawhide (which tightens as it dries), the axe-head was ready for use. These flat, tanged Egyptian axes were manufactured using a single stone mould, open

Right: An archer, with arrows and bow, carries a semi-circular axe as a secondary weapon. He tucks the haft into his belt, a common practice.

Below: Styles of later axe head. *Bottom*: Crescent-shaped tanged axe from the Middle Kingdom. *Middle*: openwork axe head (New Kingdom). *Top*: Narrow penetrating axe head (New Kingdom).

to the sky, into which the molten bronze (a mixture of copper and tin) would be poured. The author has experimented with bronze axe casting, and within only a few minutes, the bronze is cool and hard and ready to remove from the mould. All the armourer need do is tip the mould upside down and gently tap its back. Some axes have to be worked out of the mould with a knife. Stray 'wings' of bronze that were created when molten bronze spilled over the edge of the axe mould (known as 'flashing') need to be cut off and the axe cleaned, sanded, and sharpened.

The socketed axe should be familiar to readers, since it is cast with an integral hole passing right through it, designed to accept the end of a wooden haft. This design is far stronger and more superior to the simple tanged axe attachment, which is the reason the method continued in use during the Iron Age, and, of course, is still with us today. Socketed designs have been found at Til Barsip in Syria and at Ur and other sites in ancient Mesopotamia. They date to the second half of the third millennium BC, a full 1,000 years before Tuthmosis III and the Battle of Megiddo. Faced with armoured opponents, the creators of these early axes gave them narrow, armour-piercing blades and a socketed attachment method, allowing the user to exert maximum killing force. Such weapons required the use of the two-part stone mould, where a complex empty shape could be formed between the two tightly fitting stones. Once liquid bronze was poured in and allowed to cool, the leather binding around the moulds was untied, the stones pulled apart, and the socketed axe revealed. After any flashing was removed, the axe-head will have required extensive cleaning, sanding, and sharpening.

Palestinian axe design reflected the Egyptian mind-set, and relied upon the tanged attachment method. The Old Testament cautions its readers about the unreliability of these axes, and the mishaps that it relates would certainly have been shared by the Egyptian infantryman:

> (When) his hand has been raised to strike with the axe to cut the tree and the (head) has slipped off from the wooden handle and it has hit his fellow man and he has died, he ... should flee ...
>
> Deuteronomy 19:5

Faced with unarmoured opponents like the desert-dwelling Bedouin, the Nubians of the south, or the Libyans of the west, the deficiencies of the Egyptian tanged axe were not greatly missed. The heavy impact and cutting action of the semi-circular or crescent-shaped blades on unprotected flesh did their job. During the New Kingdom and following the Egyptian experience in battle with the Canaanite Hyksos forces, axe design changed. There was now a need for an axe that could challenge an armoured opponent, wearing a helmet, linen banding, or a shirt of scale armour. The Egyptian response was not to adopt the socketed axe, however, but instead to alter the shape of the blade to suit this new tactical consideration. Blades became rectangular and, during the Nineteenth Dynasty, longer and narrower. Yet the tanged fixing remained. Each axe-head retained a curved cutting edge, and, at its rear, the axe splayed out; these two projecting 'lugs' gave the rawhide bindings something to grip.

A large number of Egyptian axe-heads have survived from the New Kingdom era, some of which have been inscribed. A fascinating example in the British Museum bears the name of Kamose, the last pharaoh of the Seventeenth Dynasty. Showing distinct signs of wear on the blade, the axe may even have played its part in the expulsion of the Hyksos princes from Egypt. No less remarkable, although used for less practical and more ceremonial purposes, is a bronze axe-head inlaid with gold in the Cairo Museum that was presented to Queen Ahhotep by her son, King Ahmose, founder of the burgeoning Eighteenth Dynasty. It shows Ahmose smiting a captured enemy, and beneath them both is a griffin. Two more utilitarian examples, also from the British Museum, are complete with their short, straight wooden hafts and tightly bound rawhide fastenings; both are inscribed with the name of Tuthmosis III, yet from their plain, unadorned, and workmanlike appearance, they were unlikely to have ever been carried by him. The royal cartouche did not simply

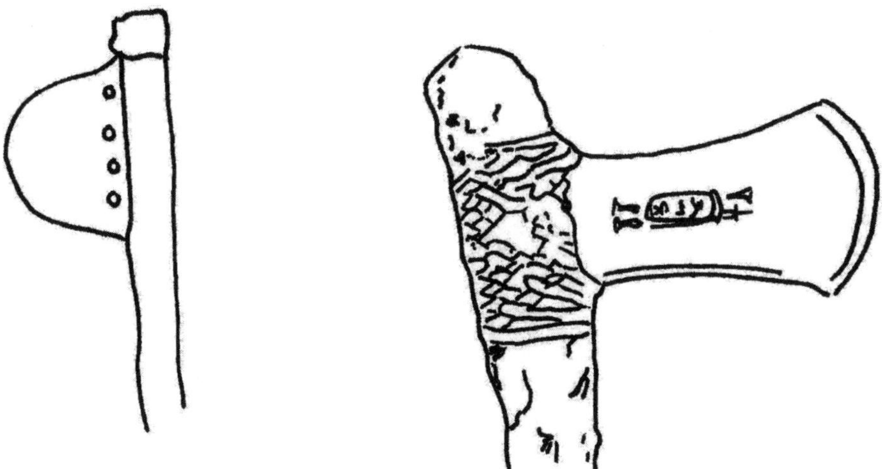

Older forms of military axe head.
Left: Semi-circular axe head of the Old Kingdom, little different from those used by Egyptian carpenters.
Right: Long, splayed axe head from the Middle Kingdom.

signify ownership—implying that any axe with the pharaoh's name actually belonged to him. The royal crest of the British monarch is worn as a badge of rank by warrant officers (class 1) in the British Army, for example, and the symbol of the royal crown is found throughout the British armed forces on badges, blazons and other insignia.

Some axes from the New Kingdom were cast in openwork, with cut-out figures or animals decorating the body of the axe-head. Such elaborations will have dramatically reduced the force of impact that a bronze axe could survive without bending or snapping and it is not known whether these weapons were ever carried into combat. A fine, hafted example in the British Museum depicts a scout on horseback.

A distinctive new type of axe grew out of the need for a more penetrating attack in order to defeat armoured opponents. The 'mace-axe' (Egyptian name unknown) did not reduce the width of the axe blade further; instead, it returned to the wide, curved blade of the Middle Kingdom crescent axe and married that to a war mace. The mace still saw service with the Egyptian army, and shipboard marines, in particular, were often depicted wielding short-handled maces complete with an integral hand guard. Here, the mace was probably constructed of a stone head that was pierced by a hole for the wooden shaft of the handle. The curved bronze blade fitted along one edge of the heavy stone head; this wide-bladed cutting axe was backed by the tremendous weight of the mace head, giving the mace-axe terrible cutting and concussive damage potential.

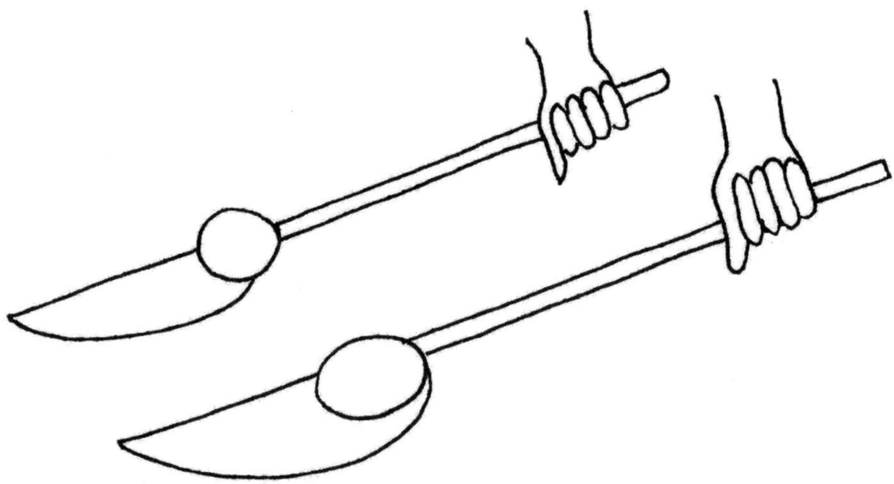

The mace-axe (Egyptian name unknown) features in several royal 'smiting scenes', but the weapon was also used by some of the infantrymen. The weapon married a wide, axe-like cutting blade with the concussive power and momentum of a heavy war mace.

The weapon is featured in a number of royal 'smiting scenes', but depictions of the mace-axe in use with the general infantrymen are quite rare. A scene from the temple of Amun at Karnak shows a soldier hefting a wooden chest on his shoulder, in his left hand he clutches both a hand-axe and a short-handled mace-axe. Both one-handed and two-handed versions must have been in use and blades for both types have been discovered. A large blade is kept in the British Museum.

Use of the Sword

> When Re made thy boundary, his two arms were a protection behind thee. Thy sword was in the midst of every land and their chiefs fell by thy blade.
>
> Relief at Karnak, reign of Seti I

Most ancient armies from the end of the seventeenth century BC onwards had adopted some form of bronze short sword, but the nature of the armies themselves, their level of training, and discipline—and the style of combat that this resulted in—prevented the weapon from being anything more than a sidearm, a back-up weapon similar to the club or the mace. These ancient armies, including the Egyptian, were generally composed of young, mainly inexperienced recruits with little military experience and a low tolerance for personal risk. Generals organised these levy troops into phalanxes of close-order spearmen that were able to defend themselves with a wall of shields, yet still threaten the enemy at spear length.

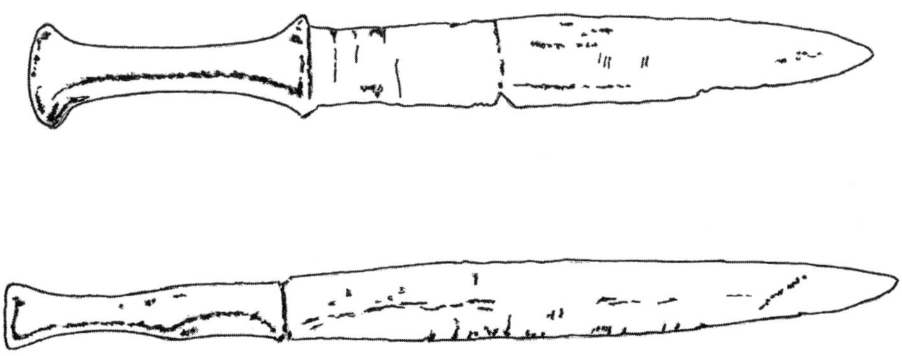

Bronze short swords from the city of Piramesse/Avaris (Nineteenth Dynasty).

The true masters of ancient swordsmanship, the men of the Roman legions, were full-time professional soldiers, with a reputation (even in their own day) for iron discipline and an unwavering courage. This steely discipline on the battlefield allowed the legionaries to brave the risks and get in close enough to use their own short sword, the gladius. For the Egyptian army to really take to the bronze sword, it would require the emergence of a unit of highly trained and motivated troops able to forgo the relative safety of the spear and shield in order to get close enough to fight with the weapon. Troops able to engage their opponents at these face-to-face ranges had also to forgo the tight pack of the phalanx since a looser formation was needed in order to give each swordsman the room that he required. Rome moved away from the phalanx and adopted the chequerboard formation based on the maniple, and curved shields were developed that protected both the front and left side of the legionary, since a 'fighting gap' had to left between each man in the formation. Roman soldiers did not, and could not, fight from behind a shield wall as they needed to get their swords past their shields and into their enemies.

Short swords, or long daggers, appear in Egyptian reliefs throughout the New Kingdom. Technological developments in bronze casting during the rule of the Hyksos had led to the invention of the Egyptian short sword with its tapered tang, which strengthened the attachment of the blade to the hilt. Some of these early cast weapons were decorated with inlaid handles and some of these handles show signs of wear, symptomatic of having being tucked into a soldier's belt—the back of the handle having rubbed against his skin or his clothing.

Swords are carried by some of the Egyptian soldiers who are besieging the Canaanite city of Ashkelon for Ramses II. One man climbs a siege ladder, sword in hand, while the other is cutting the throat of a prostrate Canaanite. Other swords are clearly carried as secondary weapons; soldiers marching in columns occasionally clutch a variety of sidearms, axes, clubs, and short swords. At times, the reliefs depict short swords thrust into a belt and carried that way, while much shorter fighting daggers are instead shown strapped to the soldier's arm in a sheath.

A more common type of bladed weapon, a curved sword or scimitar, was also carried by Egyptian units into battle. The Egyptian word for this curved sword was *khopesh*. This word means 'the foreleg of an animal', and is similar in meaning to the English expression 'dogleg'—a reference to the changing direction of the blade. Although it does resemble a sword somewhat, being a long bronze blade mounted on to a handle, the *khopesh* was actually single-edged and used only for cutting or chopping. In this way, it was utilised in much the same way as that old Egyptian standby: the axe. *Khopesh* are depicted at all levels of the Egyptian army, even being wielded by a number of New Kingdom pharaohs to smite foes on their monumental reliefs. The earliest representation of the weapon among Egyptian troops comes from the reliefs of soldiers at Queen Hatshepsut's

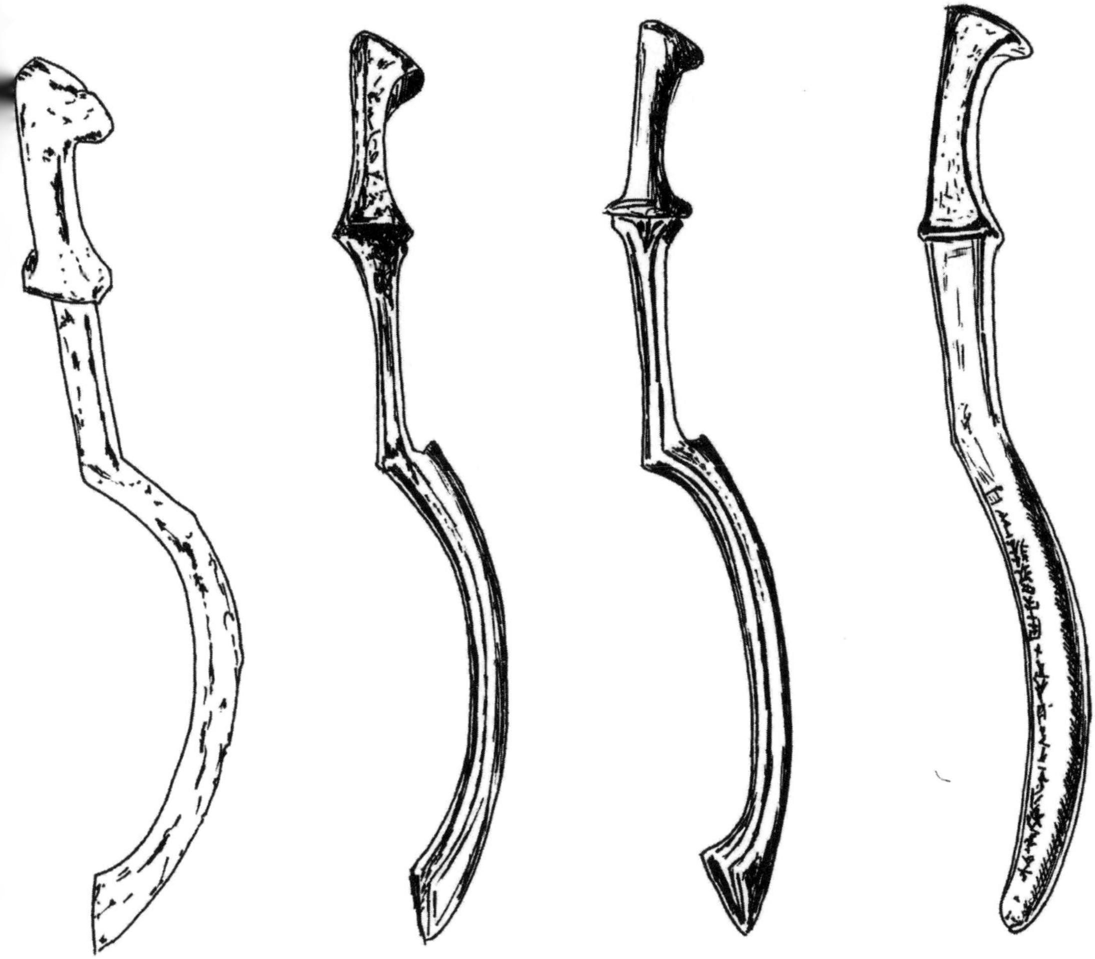

The *khopesh* or Bronze Age scimitar varied little from kingdom to kingdom. These examples are all dated to the fourteenth century BC and show a remarkable similarity of form despite being separated geographically. The Egyptian army adopted the Canaanite *khopesh* without modification. *From left to right*: *khopesh* of Adad-Nirari, king of Assyria; *khopesh* of Tutankhamun; *khopesh* from Ugarit; and *khopesh* from the Palestinian city of Gezer, in the foothills of the Judaean Mountains.

temple at Deir el-Bahri. Just like clubs and short swords, *khopesh* were secondary to the spear, they were a backup weapon used when fighting took place outside of the spear formation. The weapon is certainly distinctive, almost resembling a European sickle or billhook; indeed, it is sometimes erroneously referred to as a 'sickle sword' in older works. This term is extremely misleading as the sickle cuts on the inside of the curved blade, whereas the *khopesh* cut on the outside of the curve (in the manner of a Middle Eastern scimitar).

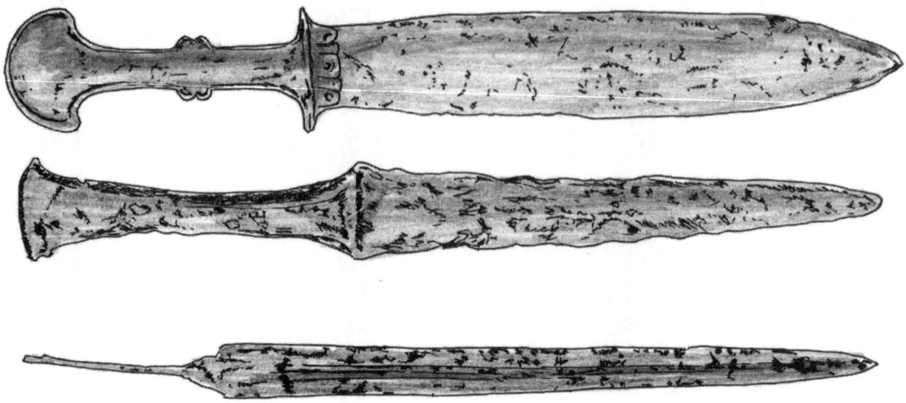

Swords of the Late Bronze Age from across the Near East. The development of the sword from dagger form to longsword is clearly seen here.
Top: Egyptian 'butter-knife-type' short sword from the fourteenth to thirteenth century BC.
Middle: 'Dagger-type' sword from Palestine, dated *c.* 1,350 BC.
Bottom: Naue Type II longsword from Ugarit, bearing the cartouche of Pharaoh Merenptah (1,224–1,214 BC); it represents a new style of slashing sword introduced by the Sea Peoples.

Sword Design

Although we use the term 'sword' (*neken*) here, the weapons were little more than short swords or long daggers. A variety of blade types were in use during the period, with most either having straight sides that tapered to a point (the classic 'dagger' shape) or blades that remained broadly parallel until they converged at a blunt or rounded tip (a 'leaf' or 'butter-knife' shape). Clearly, the first type of sword was utilised as a stabbing weapon, while the second was more of a cutting or hacking blade—the wide blade undoubtedly designed to resist bending as it was brought down hard on to an enemy's body. Some examples of the 'butter-knife' design were found at Amarna and now reside in the Cairo Museum; they were cast from bronze in a single piece—blade and hilt together. Although this used more bronze and was probably more costly, it must have tackled head-on the problem of attaching the blade to the hilt. Other short swords had wooden hilts and one beautiful 'dagger-shaped' sword in the British Museum (dated to the start of the Eighteenth Dynasty) has a wooden hilt gilded with gold, perhaps qualifying it as a gift from pharaoh to one of his troops—the oft-mentioned 'gold of valour'. The blade of this particular example featured a strengthening mid-rib and its shape resembled, almost exactly, various gold-bladed short swords from the Mesopotamian city of Ur and dated to 1,000 years earlier. Unlike these Mesopotamian examples, however, the Egyptian example featured a semi-circular pommel. This pommel design is found on most of the extant Egyptian swords in collections today. Had the Egyptian sword shape been copied, through intermediaries, from the Sumerians?

The *khopesh* was certainly an import and had its origins in ancient Mesopotamia—a number of examples have been found that date from the very beginning of the second millennium BC. From there, it was adopted very quickly by the city-states of Syria and Canaan and only later, after the Hyksos interregnum, by the Egyptians. These early antecedents were composed of a handgrip to which was attached a long bronze blade with a mid-rib. The final half of the blade curved out in the form of a 'C'. The weapon had evolved from a shallow crescent axe design and it continued to excel as a heavy chopping weapon.

By the time the *khopesh* had entered Egyptian arsenals, the design had evolved again. The straight part of the blade had become shorter and the curved 'C' element had grown in length; however, the overall length of the weapon remained unchanged. It was, after all, the curved blade that did the damage, and by lengthening this section of the blade, the *khopesh* could inflict longer and more serious wounds on its victim. Throughout the kingdoms of the Near East, the design of the scimitar was broadly similar. Two examples of the Egyptian *khopesh* were found within the tomb of Tutankhamun and show a remarkable similarity to other scimitars recovered from Ugarit, Gezer, and Asshur. The popularity of this bladed weapon increased during the New Kingdom, reaching a peak, studies suggest, during the reign of Pharaoh Merenptah in the second half of the Nineteenth Dynasty. By this time, the curved *khopesh* and the straight short sword appear with equal regularity on military themed reliefs, although the short sword does feature more heavily in scenes of direct violence, whereas the *khopesh* tends to feature more in secondary, ceremonial, or non-combat roles. Was this an artistic convention? Or did it reflect an actual division of operational use between the two hand weapons?

The Sword of the Sea Peoples

While the Egyptian short swords (*neken*) were specialised weapons that excelled either at thrusting or cutting, longer swords capable of being used to perform either method of attack would enter Egypt during the late Nineteenth Dynasty. The *Shardana*, Ramses II's elite mercenary troops, are shown during the Battle of Kadesh carrying both a circular shield and a short stabbing sword, similar if not identical to the 'dagger-style' short sword. Unlike their Egyptian comrades, the *Shardana* sometimes sheath these swords in scabbards that are strapped to the chest. Another relief from the same period depicts the storming of a city, and *Shardana* there wield unusually long swords. These long, stabbing rapiers appear again in reliefs dedicated to the victories of Pharaoh Ramses III—most seem to reach almost 1 metre in length.

Other Sea Peoples were equally enamoured of the stabbing sword; *Peleset* warriors, who fought in the great land battle of 1,187 BC, all carry dagger-like short swords. However, the invaders who were involved in the Delta sea battle instead have long rapiers. The artist really emphasises these weapons; they are long and broad, almost impossibly so, but the point is made—these *Peleset* and *Shekelesh* fight with longswords that dwarf the Egyptian short sword. Libyan warriors also carry this rapier with them during their own Nile incursions, not in limited numbers as one might expect from a nomadic desert-dwelling people, but in prodigious numbers. Pharaoh Merenptah reported that his victorious troops were able to seize 9,111 swords from his Libyan foes, almost equal in number to the number of enemy killed. Merenptah helpfully provides us with a scribal tally of severed hands and penises collected in the aftermath of the battle; it amounted to a casualty figure of 9,724. Did every man have a bronze rapier? Where did these weapons come from?

Long thrusting rapiers were current in the Eastern Mediterranean from the sixteenth century BC onwards and fine examples have been found in Bronze Age Greece and Turkey that certainly seem to match the length and shape of the *Shardana* blades. One preserved blade, discovered at Bêt Dagin near Gaza in 1910, is known simply as the '*Shardana* sword' and is believed to have been made and used by *Peleset* warriors who settled in Palestine following their abortive attacks on the Nile Delta. The weakness in these rapiers comes not just from their narrow blades themselves, but also from the inadequate, flimsy tangs that must have done little to stop the blade snapping away from the handle during combat.

A new type of bronze sword, known to archaeologists as the Naue Type II or the *Griffzungenschwert*, began to appear throughout the Eastern Mediterranean around 1,200 BC. Like many of the native Egyptian swords, the Naue II was cast in a single piece, but it was much longer—examples are around 70 cm in length. The blades of these swords are characterised by straight, parallel sides tapering to a sharp point. At the opposite end, a flat, strong tang is often present, complete with rivet holes by which method wooden or bone grips would have been attached to the sword. It is obvious from the shape of the Naue II blade that the sword could be used effectively for both stabbing and slashing, and with its centre of gravity much farther down the blade than with other sword designs of this era, a cutting blow had greater velocity and much greater force.

The Naue Type II was introduced to the kingdoms and city-states of the Eastern Mediterranean around 1,200 BC, although it had been in use throughout central and northern Europe for almost two centuries. This was its place of origin. For the first time in Near Eastern history, military technology had arrived west from Europe rather than east from Mesopotamia. This new type of longsword, manufactured in both bronze and iron, does not appear in Egyptian reliefs of the period, yet examples have been found across the Eastern Mediterranean, including Cyprus, mainland Greece, Crete, and Syria. Of greatest interest to us is the so-called Merenptah sword, found buried in a cache within the walls of the Syrian city of Ugarit. Newly cast, the sword was unsharpened and marked with the royal cartouche of Merenptah himself. It is 74 cm long and has the parallel blade of a Naue sword, some 4cm wide at the mid-point. Archaeologists have speculated that the sword was part of a consignment cast on behalf of the pharaoh and destined to be shipped to Egypt. Unfortunately for the people of Ugarit, raiders were sighted out at sea and the city was sacked soon after. A clay writing tablet was discovered at Ugarit, still within the oven that was to bake it, and that tablet carried the message that raiding ships had just been spotted off the coast. When the city was razed to the ground soon after by these raiders, this tablet was inadvertently fired and survived the millennia to bear witness to the final moments of the doomed city. The Merenptah sword was not a *Shardana*-style rapier, it was both a thrusting and cutting weapon; it was very similar to the revolutionary European Naue Type II swords, but lacked the wide riveted tang, instead tapering to a thin unriveted tang that would have provided little long-term strength to the weapon in combat. Whatever the armament and logistical plans of Merenptah, the Egyptian forces never did adopt the longsword and the native troops of the companies and divisions continued to use the tried and tested weaponry of the New Kingdom that had served them so well down the centuries.

8

Ranged Weapons

(His Majesty) pulled the bow while holding four arrows in his hand. He rode northward, firing at them, like Montu in his battle-dress, each arrow piercing the back of the target as he fired at the next. This deed had never been done—shooting an arrow at a target of copper, so that it came out (of the other side) and fell to the earth.

Relief dated to Amenhotep II

For most armies of the ancient world, ranged weapons, like slings and bows, served as an adjunct, a supporting arm of long-range skirmishers that provided covering and harassment fire on behalf of a mainly infantry army. Egypt had always placed a special emphasis on its missile troops, however, and on a corps of archers in particular. Bows were used not just by the elite chariot warriors, but also by dedicated infantry archers (*megau*, or 'shooters').

There were other ranged weapons in use during the New Kingdom, in particular javelins (which were discussed in the last chapter), slings, and throwsticks.

Archery

When the composite bow was introduced into Egypt by the Hyksos warlords, it did not wholly eclipse the native self bow, which continued in use throughout the New Kingdom. A number of lemonwood self bows—each unstrung and 1.8 metres in length—were recovered from the tomb of royal fan-bearer Ahmose Penhat at Deir el-Bahri. Yet the new and more powerful composite bow had greater penetrative power and inflicted far more serious wounds at longer ranges, making it the standard military bow of the age. However, a number of varying designs were adopted, each perhaps an attempt at improvement on the Canaanite original. Three main designs appear in military reliefs: the first takes the shape of a double concave (or 'recurve'); the second design resembles a Western bow, with the bow stave generally remaining straight along its length, curving back at the tips; and a third type of bow is distinctly angular, the arms are straight and meet at the handgrip (at an angle of around 120 degrees) to form the shape of a 'V' when strung.

Recurved bows are seen being used in archery instruction on wall paintings within the tomb of Menna, while the curved bow is carried by a unit of archers on the painted chest of Tutankhamun. Shaven headed archers armed with the angular bow appear at Ramses III's mortuary temple at Medinet Habu and detail from the tomb of Menkheperrasonb illustrates activity within an archery workshop. In it, one man is shaving wood off of a bow stave with a carpenter's adze, another is splitting wood with a saw, and one craftsman tests the pull of an angular bow, while his colleague checks the straightness of a reed arrow. The angular bow seems to be a more advanced design.

Composite bows were generally around 1.5 metres in length and manufactured from several separate materials (as the name implies). In this way, they differed radically from the Egyptian single-piece self bow as well as the medieval long bow. Composite bows were built up of layers of wood and horn, stuck together with strong natural glues. In a text from the Syrian city of Ugarit, Aqhat promises to provide the necessary bow-making products to Anat:

> Let me vow tqbm (birch wood?) from Lebanon
> Let me vow tendons from wild bulls
> Let me vow horns from wild goats
> Sinews from the locks of bulls.

Not all the bows in use by the divisions and companies had been manufactured in local military workshops, though. Just like scale armour, composite bows

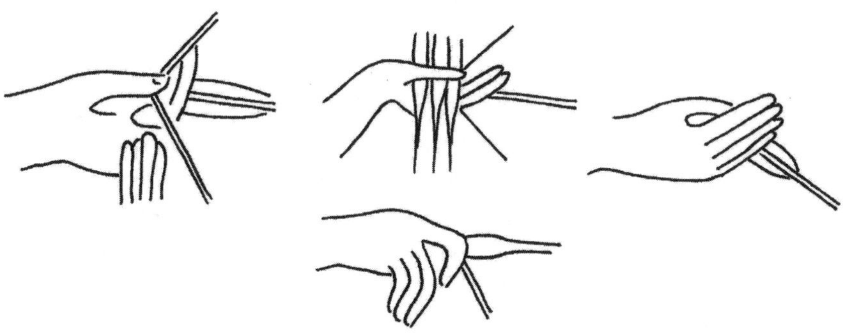

Methods of drawing the arrow, from various Egyptian reliefs.

could be received as tribute from subject peoples. In a world without money, goods themselves were wealth and it was more advantageous to have foreign workers send good quality bows to Egypt, then send gold or silver that pharaoh would then use to pay for the construction of bows locally. Ramses III was able to bring back 603 composite bows from his successful campaign against the Libyans. Not just the archery corps of Ramses III, but also his personal entourage, the royal princes, and the army's chariot warriors all carried these expensive and prestigious pieces of equipment.

Archers are not actively depicted in the major battle reliefs, although, where they do appear, they march in formation or string their bows while they wait for battle to begin. Portrayals of siege operations do give the archer a more active role; he is often portrayed shooting a volley of arrows in support of combat infantrymen. In the aftermath of war, archers seem to have been used for the counting and guarding of prisoners and some seem to carry coils of rope that may have been carried for that very purpose. Does this mean that archers were of lower status than hand-to-hand fighters? In an interesting parallel, English longbowmen at the Battle of Agincourt in 1415 were ordered to kill some of the French prisoners when the battle looked to be in question. In that instance, it is likely that the more noble, higher status men-at-arms would have refused to perform such a cowardly task. Why the Egyptian archers were earmarked for such assignments is unknown—perhaps the range of the bow allowed the archers to take down fleeing prisoners at a distance.

During the Eighteenth Dynasty, units of archers carrying curved or recurved bows are shown with the weapons sloped over one shoulder, as a spearman might do with his own weapon. Quivers were not a common part of the archer's kit during this earlier period; instead, the soldiers typically clutch arrows in their right hand as they march. The colourful painted figures on Tutankhamun's box are shown to carry their ammunition in this way. Quivers that do appear are roughly tubular, wide-mouthed affairs, capable of carrying scores of arrows. One chariot, being prepared for an expedition to Palestine, is recorded as being equipped with a well-stocked quiver of eighty arrows. Infantry quivers would not have been that capacious. Medieval longbowmen carried around twenty-five to thirty arrows within their quivers and could carry multiple quivers on to the battlefield. The author, who has been a member of an archery club and shot arrows many times from a Roman composite bow in full armour, would have to assess the capacity of the New Kingdom quivers as portrayed in the reliefs at about thirty arrows. Continual replenishment of arrows during a battle would be crucial to victory. From the contemporary records of Nuzi, a city within ancient Mesopotamia, a clay tablet records a list of military kit: '5 leather quivers, 30 arrows in each … total 7 leather quivers, 178 arrows placed in them'.

Most archery quivers were made of leather, although a number are known to have been constructed from woven plant fibres. Quivers became more elaborately decorated during the Nineteenth and Twentieth Dynasties and were often embossed with floral designs and coloured with leather dyes. Square-shaped leather lids for the quivers were used to protect the delicate fletchings of the arrows and were attached by leather thongs. Other innovative ways of carrying arrows and bows sometimes appear on the reliefs. On reliefs within the tomb of Pharaoh Horemheb, for example, a set of cylindrical quivers hang from a carrier, while a group of archers fighting for Ramses III appear at Medinet Habu carrying their quivers of arrows with a hand strap. One of the shaven-headed archers at Medinet Habu even wears his angular bow across his chest, held in place by a fabric sling thrown over his shoulder—similar perhaps to a Native American papoose. In combat, quivers were stood upright in front of the archer, from where he could pluck arrows with ease. Often the quivers are shown in pairs, suggesting that the soldiers carried two or more quivers with them into battle.

Some Eighteenth Dynasty archers wrapped a length of leather or cloth around the central section of the strung bow, although the reason for this practice is obscure. Perhaps it was meant as a method of protecting the bow from the ravages of direct sunlight (moisture, the real killer of composite bows, would certainly not have been a factor in the Near East). Triangular bow cases were used by some archers to fully protect their weapons, and these cases were decorated according to the means of their owners. Bow cases are illustrated on reliefs from the tombs of Kenamun, Huy, and Meri, and we are lucky enough

A variety of quiver shapes are seen in use here by archers of Ramses III's army. On the far left, the quiver is secured with a cloth sling, and this technique is used by the central archer to carry his bow. This figure also has an animal-headed quiver lid.

to have a single surviving example from the tomb of Tutankhamun. Composite bows were complex devices that required particular care or else they could be permanently ruined. The author knows of one Roman re-enactment group that commissioned the construction of a couple of authentic laminated wood-and-horn composite bows for use in public displays. One was left strung over the course of a weekend and this destroyed the bow's inherent springiness—it no longer wanted to return to its 'at rest' position. The second bow was also strung, but left out in the sun on a searingly hot August afternoon—it also lost its power and flexibility. Moisture and damp conditions would also prove to be the enemy of the composite bow as we have already mentioned, which is the reason that they were popular weapons in the eastern Mediterranean. In the west, meanwhile, the flat bow and later the longbow found more favour. Bow cases were strapped to the sides of war chariots along with quivers full of arrows and javelins.

Bow strings were made of animal gut, and a number of examples were found inside a surviving archer's kit—a linen cloth wrapped around spare bow strings, a leather wrist-guard, and lumps of malachite, perhaps for darkening the skin around the eyes to cut down glare from the sun. One string, recovered with the slain soldiers of Montuhotep II, was made of twisted gut 240 mm in length and it was found to be 2 mm thick. Bow strings were also made of strips of linen. In the tomb of Baqt III at Beni Hasan, a soldier is depicted in the act of stringing his bow, knee bent with his leg between the string and the bent bow stave, a technique the author has also used when stringing later designs of composite bow.

Baqt's tomb also portrays archers roaming the battlefield following a successful attack, picking up spent arrows and pulling them from the bodies of casualties. Egyptian arrows were traditionally made of lengths of Nile reed—they were light and strong and were made to accept to short wooden tip onto which the killing point was attached. Where the wooden 'foreshaft' and the main reed shaft met, the archer used thread or sinew to bind them and black mastic to then strengthen the join. Most surviving arrows range in length between 559 and 864 mm, although they could reach up to 1 metre. In the New Kingdom, the business end of the arrow was typically tipped with a triangular or barbed and socketed or tanged bronze head. Three feathers were used to fletch each arrow, equally spaced and glued in place around the end of the shaft. A large number of tanged New Kingdom arrowheads were recovered from Piramesse by Manfred Bietak that range dramatically in length and style.

In warfare, archers had a number of roles: as the guards for contingents of prisoners, as supporting troops for siege operations, as frontline combat troops, and as scouts. Army commanders put archers into a forward line ahead of the hand-to-hand fighters. Withering volleys of accurate arrow shot could be directed at the enemy frontline during the approach to contact, and following

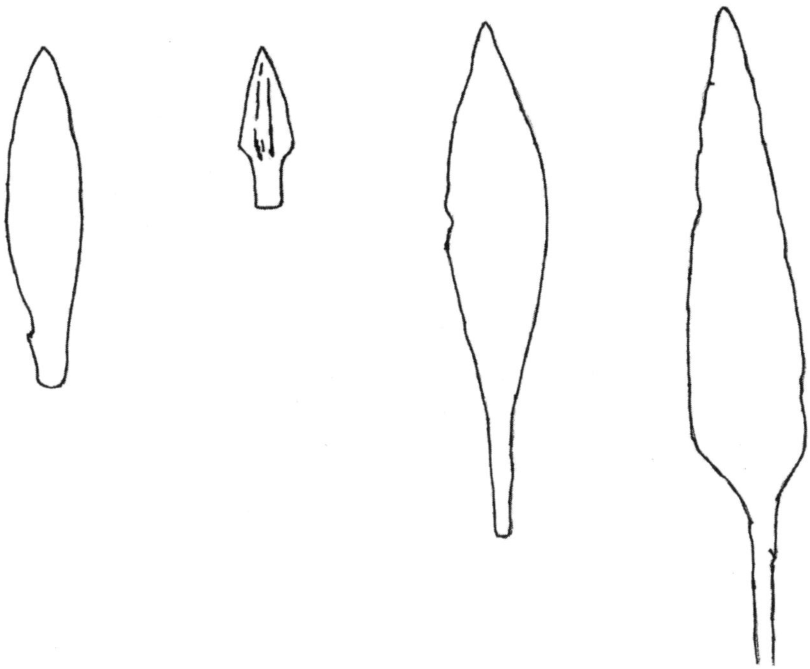

Tanged arrowheads from the city of Piramesse/Avaris (Nineteenth Dynasty).

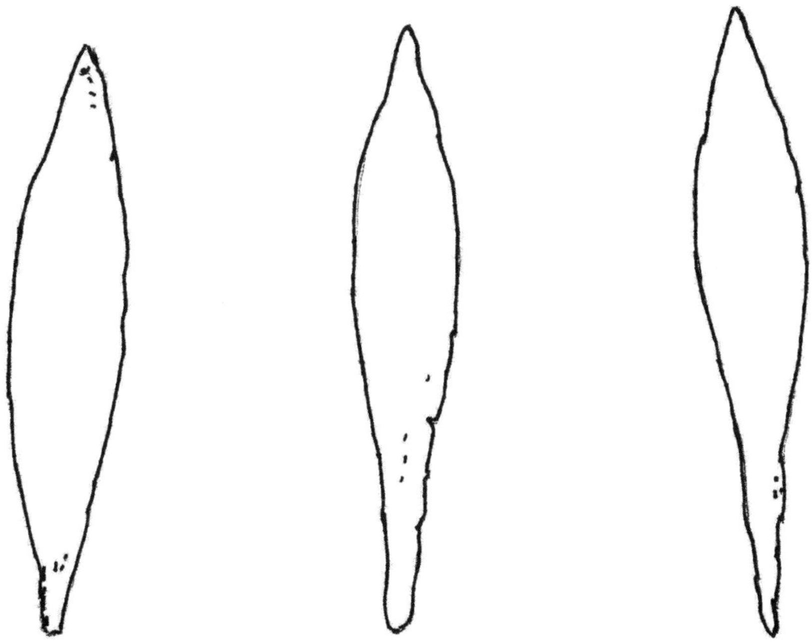

Tanged arrowheads from the city of Piramesse/Avaris (Nineteenth Dynasty).

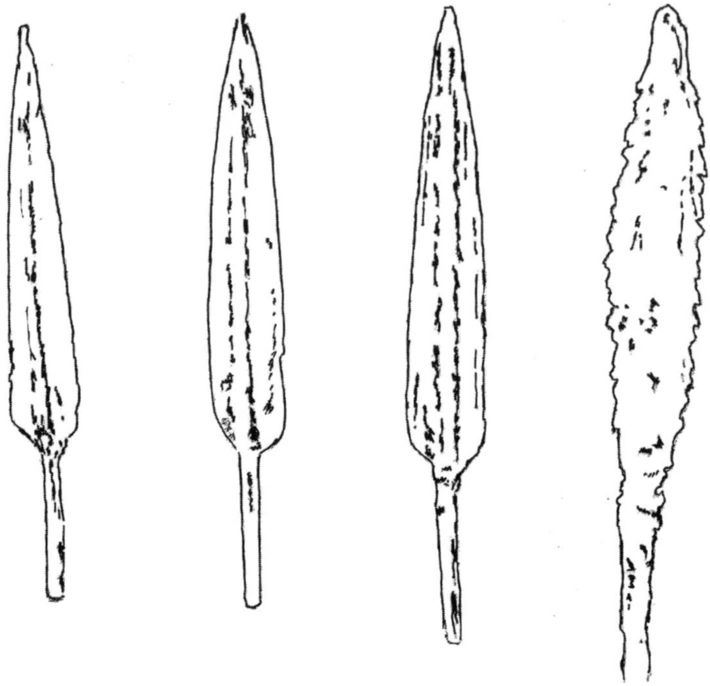

Tanged arrowheads from the city of Piramesse/Avaris (Nineteenth Dynasty).

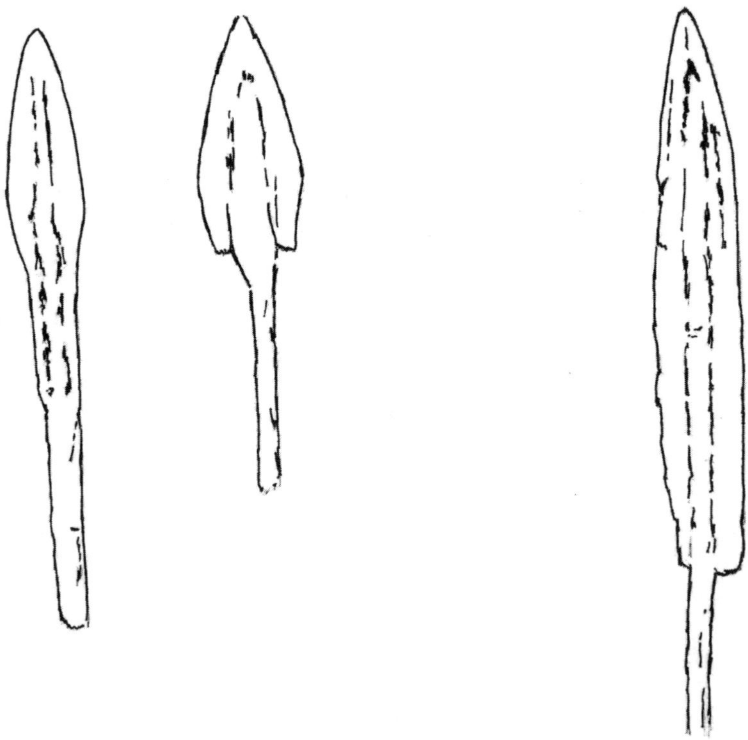

this, with the archers now in the rear, this aerial attack could continue to strike at the many body of the enemy unit even as the Egyptian spearmen and axemen entered the fight. With a preponderance of archers, the New Kingdom army might have been tempted to fight defensively from behind the safety of a barrier, but there is little evidence for this. The Egyptian army typically moved aggressively to contact, with bowmen provided a shock supporting element.

Some estimates of the capabilities of Egyptian self bows suggest an accurate range of between 50–60 metres. The composite bow was able to project an arrow out to range of 250–300 metres. Watching experienced archers shooting replica composite bows, however, the author noted that a point-and-shoot range for the bow should be more realistically set at around 100 metres. Typical speeds for arrows shot from this kind of bow average around 80 kph and can penetrate as much as 7.5 cm of flesh. The simple textile banding worn as body armour by Egyptian soldiers was probably an attempt to reduce some of the penetrative power of the enemy's arrows, rather than protect against axe blades and spear points.

Finally, it should be noted that dogs are sometimes shown in the company of archers, suggestive of scouting and reconnaissance for which hunting dogs would prove eminently suitable. Some of the royal bodyguards are shown in the company of dogs and there were certainly military kennels at the great fort of Buhen, whose Egyptian troops patrolled the Nubian frontier. Some scouts or messengers are shown on horseback, a radical new tactical innovation and these fast-moving scouts carried a bow and wore a quiver of arrows on their back.

Slings

The sling was an ancient weapon that had been used by shepherds and mountain-folk for centuries. It was no more than a pouch of leather or woven textile connected to two cords at either end. Whipped over the head at great speed, a stone could be discharged with incredible force. Some slings were alternatively made of woven plant fibre or animal hair, depending on the people making them and the materials available to them. The Egyptian army made little use of the sling, although there are a handful of reliefs that depict slingers in action. It is unlikely that these soldiers represent native Egyptian troops, rather they are most likely to be nomad mercenaries, Bedouin from Canaan or the Eastern Desert, where the sling was prized not just as a shepherd's defence against wolves, but also as a hunting weapon. As late as the nineteenth century AD, slings were still being used in Egypt to drive away birds from corn fields. The army, however, had enjoyed a tradition of archery for centuries, and the sling could not easily compete with the power and accuracy of the ubiquitous composite bow.

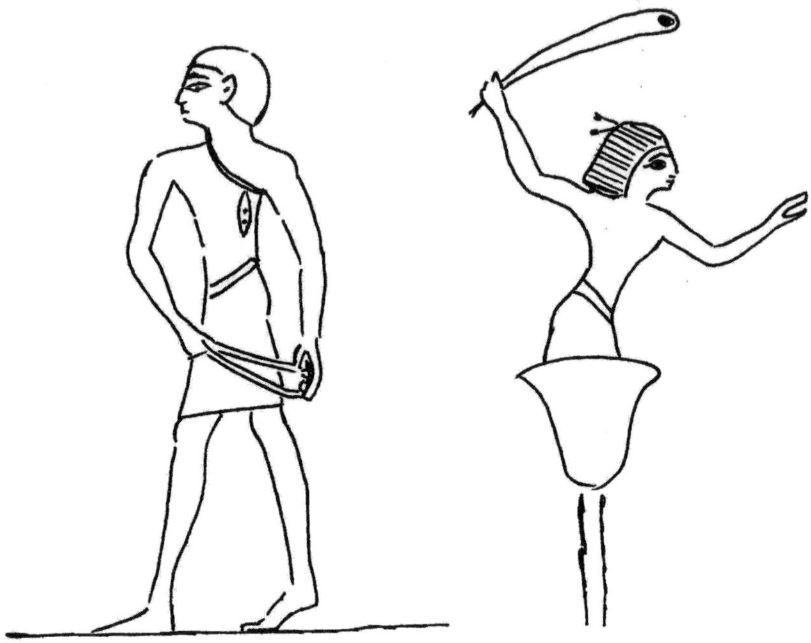

Slingers in action. Archery eclipsed the sling in Egyptian warfare, yet the weapon was in use.
Left: An Egyptian slinger.
Right: Naval slinging in action, this marine hurls stones from the crow's nest of a ship.

Slingers are depicted at Beni Hasan, as well as in the crow's nest of an Egyptian warship during the Twentieth Dynasty naval battle against the Sea Peoples. Why the Egyptian crew would post a slinger at the mast-top to act as a sniper, hurling down high-velocity stones onto the enemy vessels is unknown.

There are four surviving Egyptian slings currently held in museum collections, with a further two slings that have possibly been misidentified. The most famous of these extant weapons are the two woven flax slings found with Tutankhamun's belongings. These sling pouches are almond in shape and gently cupped, ready to hold the sling stone ammunition. It is widely supposed that these slings were part of the young pharaoh's hunting gear.

Two flax slings were found at el-Lahun (el-Lahun is in Upper Egypt, close to the Faiyum and is also known as Kahun). One is dated from the Third Intermediate Period, a time of foreign usurpation, which followed the New Kingdom. It is in the Petrie Museum, London, and has a rhomboid-shaped woven pouch with braided cords. The pouch is 125×70 mm and what is left of the only remaining cord measures 570 mm in length. The cord is about 6 mm square in section. The total length of the original sling, assuming that no parts of the fragmentary cord are missing, would have been around 1,270 mm. The second Lahun sling is currently in the Manchester Museum, it has a slightly dished pouch and cords of twisted flax. It dates from the Twelfth Dynasty of the Middle Kingdom. Two other objects were found together with Tutankhamun's funerary items that were identified as 'belts', but that are clearly slings. Both feature almond-shaped, woven pouches with quite thin, braided cords attached at either end.

The author has made replicas of various leather Roman slings and become quite proficient in their use. The pouches are around 150 mm long, and the two leather cords are 600 mm long. One cord ends in a loop that fits over the index finger, the other cord ends in a knot that is pinched between thumb and forefinger. This finger loop is found on some of the Egyptian slings. To release the stone during a sling, the knot is released and the stone flies toward the target. Two things become immediately clear when one begins to practise with the sling; it is a deadly weapon worthy of respect and it takes a huge amount of practise to become even moderately proficient in its use. Slinging smooth pebbles out to 70 or 80 metres becomes fairly easy relatively quickly, but hitting a human-sized target at anything beyond 20 metres is a little more difficult. For a unit of Egyptian mercenary slingers, accuracy would not have been a great concern. The objective for the unit as a whole would have been to cast their sling

An Egyptian slinger readies his weapon, he has a bag over his shoulder within which he carries his sling stone ammunition.

stones and simply hit the enemy formation—obviously a large and relatively immobile target. Even troops with minimal training would have been able to achieve this.

Difficulties arise when slinging at distance, in bad weather, or for accuracy. Contrary to a popular misconception, the sling is not whirled around the head at fantastic speed before being released. After only three revolutions the sling stone has already reached its maximum potential speed and further spinning just ruins the slinger's aim. Everything hangs on the timing of the release. In fact, through experimentation, the author has found that a single 'snap' motion provides a good deal of accuracy and power.

> They should also be accustomed to rotating the sling once only about the head, when the stone is discharged from it.
>
> Vegetius
> *Epitome of Military Science*

The slinger can attempt one of three broad styles: overhead, overarm, and underarm. Very likely the trainer passed on the slinging method that he himself had first been taught. Using smooth beach pebbles, the author noticed that it was difficult to increase accuracy because each stone was of a slightly different shape, a different weight, and often a different density. Despite a consistent and methodical slinging style, the variations in the stones created slight variation in accuracy. Sling stones were notoriously invisible in flight, unlike arrows, and they could not be dodged or easily defended against. In addition, sling stones were not affected by cross-winds as the fletchings on arrows were, although slinging in any kind of wind is difficult because the thongs tend to spin and tangle during reloading.

Throwsticks

A weapon appears in the reliefs that resembles in shape a short, bent stick—this is not an attempt at representing a war club, but it is an Egyptian throwing stick. It seems an unlikely weapon, appearing primarily in hunting scenes, where it is used to bring down water fowl. Throwsticks were eminently suited to this type of target, the spinning stick had a good chance of catching the wing of an escaping bird and only a slight impact would be enough to stun the animal until it could be recovered by the hunter or his dog. Range and penetrating ability were not important and neither was the encumbering nature of the stick. In some scenes, the hunter's son stands ready to hand extra throwsticks to his father.

Although they do not appear frequently in the hands of soldiers, throwsticks are sometimes seen in military contexts. A column of troops on the temple walls at Deir el-Bahri, for example, clutch an axe in one hand and a throwstick in the other. In addition, Canaanite infantryman are sometimes depicted with the weapon. What was its military purpose? There were many drawbacks to the throwstick: it was large and bulky; it had a short range; it had none of the penetrating power of the arrow or javelin; and it lacked the incredible velocity of the sling stone. Yet it must have had some redeeming features.

In fact, the throwsticks found with burials are made of heavy, hard wood and are often shaped and flattened to offer a narrow profile and less resistance as they spun through the air. This will have extended the range of the throwstick beyond what one would normally expect, particularly in the hands of a strong and skilled thrower. Recovered specimens vary from 350 mm to 600 mm in length and have a breadth of around 35 mm. In shape, they curve at the mid-point or close to the tip. Many throwsticks have been found with leather or string bindings around their middle that served as simple hand grips. The author's own trials with a relatively straight throwstick of similar dimensions yielded ranges between 20 metres and 30 metres.

Obviously, a weapon like this could not be used to pick off targets at a distance, such as sentries on a parapet. It could also not be used by soldiers to attack the rear ranks of an enemy formation. It is most likely that the throwstick was used to attack the front rank of an enemy formation at ranges of 30 metres or less. Roman legionaries attempted to break up the charge of an on-coming force with a volley of heavy weight javelins and the throwstick could easily have performed a similar function. Here, the weapon's lack of killing power and its short range will have been mitigated by its shock impact. A volley of throwsticks hurled at a phalanx of unarmoured or lightly armoured enemy may have cracked skulls and fractured arms. It will have had the effect of forcing them behind their shields, slowing their charge, and perhaps breaking up the oncoming formation.

9

Military Operations

I sailed (with Tuthmosis I) when he ascended the river to Khenthennofer in order to cast out violence in the highlands, in order to suppress the raiding of the hill region. I showed bravery in his presence in the bad water in the passage of the ship by the bend. (He) appointed me chief of sailors.

Inscription of Ahmose, son of Ebana

New Kingdom Egypt was wealthy, sophisticated, civilised, and technologically advanced. In warfare, this technological development gave the army the ability to engage in new and effective types of operations. Pre-eminent among these military operations was the investment and overthrow of fortified cities, amphibious attack and marine transport, and the use of chariot squadrons on the battlefield.

Chariot Tactics

Infantry were always vulnerable to the attacks of chariotry. For the spearmen standing in close formation, an oncoming charge of horse-drawn chariots represented a threat that could not easily be countered. Chariot tactics in the ancient Near East did not rely on chariots physically smashing into formed-up phalanxes of hostile troops, instead they focused on harassing the infantry with a large volume of arrow shot before wheeling away to safety. Hittite chariot forces, however, seem to have gotten in closer and attacked their enemies with spears, much like a medieval knight fighting from his charger. Although the Kadesh reliefs usually show Hittite horses as unarmoured, those at Abu Simbel depict the chariot horses wearing scale coats ('barding') over a textile trapper. This, as well as the Hittite tactic of adding an extra crewman to these heavy Hittite chariots, further added to the chariot's effectiveness for close-combat attack. Some historians doubt the ability of a soldier to attack men on the ground with a spear and believe that Hittite chariots were employed in the same manner as were the Canaanite *maryannu*, i.e. as archery platforms. However, there is plenty of evidence from Bronze Age Greece that the chariot warriors there fought with long spears and not bows. Troops from the Land of Hatti were practising a form of warfare that existed either side of the Aegean Sea. Carrying a crew of three meant that the Hittite vehicle was sturdier, but heavier and less manoeuvrable than its Canaanite and Egyptian counter-parts.

Tactical deliberation before the Battle of Megiddo by Tuthmosis II and his generals weighed the threat of taking the long route to the city, against the short route through the pass of Aruna. This hinged on the fear of attack by enemy chariots should the Canaanites get wind of the Egyptian arrival before the army could deploy for battle. Unformed and unprepared, the weary troops would have been easy prey for the 'fire and manoeuvre' tactics of the enemy chariot force. This was where the chariot excelled. Likewise, at the Battle of Kadesh, the greatest damage inflicted upon the Egyptian army was the initial chariot assault against the division of Ra as it marched across the plain in front of the city towards its encampment. Troops of the Ra division fled in blind, disorganised panic, pursued and harassed by the heavy three-man chariots of King Muwatalis. According to the reliefs that record the battle, these chariots then broke into the Egyptian camp and wreaked havoc there. This was always the primary role of cavalry in the ancient world (once it was adopted) to exploit a weakness in an enemy formation and to move rapidly to strike at men on foot when they were unprepared or fleeing.

Today, the popular image of cavalry on the battlefield is of a force that charges head-on into quaking infantrymen, yet this rarely occurred, the horse being unwilling to gallop into a mass of men, particularly one armed with spears or bayonets. At the Battle of Waterloo, fought in 1815, Ensign Rees Gronow later related how 'the horses of the first rank of cuirassiers, in spite of all the efforts of their riders, came to a standstill, shaking and covered with foam, at about twenty yards distance.... And generally resisted all attempts to force them to charge the line of serried steel'. Another British officer described how a squadron of French cavalrymen failed even to urge their horses over the bodies of their comrades that lay dead in front of the British positions. Chariot troops in the ancient world will have faced the same challenges when faced by aggressive and well-ordered infantry. Chariots seem to have excelled at harassment and at exploiting disorder, panic, or tactical ineptitude.

The development of the Egyptian war chariot was a response to the threat posed by enemy vehicles and it served as an anti-chariot weapon. Being light and fast, the Egyptian design was able to scout ahead of the main body of troops yet still return at speed to protect the infantry from an enemy chariot attack. It is clear from the Kadesh reliefs at Abu Simbel that Egyptian chariots charged line abreast towards a line of Hittite chariots. Individual vehicles would have been well-spaced, primarily to pass through the enemy squadron rather than crash directly into it, but also to allow for a rapid 180-degree turn once that line had been penetrated. A flurry of arrows would be loosed by the chariot warrior (*seneny*) at the approaching chariots and so archery skills formed a crucial part of training for chariot crews. An account that describes the training regime of Amenhotep II celebrates his accuracy with the bow while his chariot horses were at full gallop. With charging chariot lines rapidly closing the distance between one another, opportunities for arrow shots were few—every arrow had to count. If enough casualties were inflicted by the Egyptian *seneny*, then the enemy might break off any further attack, allowing the Egyptians to carry out their turn and then aggressively pursue the survivors.

If not, then the rival chariot squadrons would engage in a confused tail-chasing melee, a dusty dogfight where javelins would be thrown, arrows shot, and, at times, clubs and spears wielded in self-defence. Chariots with a rapid rate of turn had the advantage here, and Egypt's lightweight designs would have been extremely agile in comparison with the heavier vehicles employed by the Mitanni and Hittites. Chariot runners (*peherer*), the fast-moving infantry that accompanied chariots into battle, were there to kill any dismounted enemy troops that had survived the initial charge. At Abydos, runners are shown killing or taking the hands from fallen enemy charioteers. They could also rescue members of their own chariot force. As both chariot lines penetrated one another, the Egyptian chariot runners knew they were about to face the enemy chariots and were ready to deal with them, using bows and javelins in an effort to hit horses and men.

Chariot Design

The heart of a chariot was its cab—a floor upon which the crew stood that had an outer frame with a covering of cowhide around the front and sides, leaving the rear of the cab free for mounting and dismounting. The frame was typically of steam-bent ash or elm wood and the hide included a large cut-out on each side in an attempt to decrease weight. Egyptian chariots were so light that they are sometimes depicted being carried upon the shoulders of tribute-bearers. The floorplan of the cab was D-shaped, wide enough only for two men to stand side by side. The Florence Museum chariot dates from the early Eighteenth Dynasty and is the earliest known Egyptian example. Its cab is 100 cm wide, 75 cm high, and 50 cm deep. The floor was not made of heavy planks of wood, but from strips of rawhide that were woven together to form a springy and lightweight platform. This acted as an efficient suspension system that was designed to make the archer's deadly work easier.

Although the wheels of the Eighteenth Dynasty Florence chariot had four spokes, this proved to be an early stage in the development of the Egyptian chariot. The chariot of Tuthmosis IV was unusually depicted with eight spokes, perhaps representing an experiment that proved inefficient. Following this date (*circa* 1,400 BC), all Egyptian chariots began to be manufactured with six spokes, and the slightly heavier and more robust chariots found within the tomb of Tutankhamun are of this design. The spokes appear at first glance to be simple lengths of wood, but they are actually complex constructions, each formed from half of a steam-shaped section of wood bent into a 'V'. These V-shaped sections of wood were glued together with the V-tip fastened to the hub by moist cattle intestines. Four V-shaped sections of wood joined to their neighbours to form four strong spokes.

Curved pieces of elm wood formed the wheel's hub, glued and bound with bronze wire. Tyres were then fitted that were made of rawhide, which was left to dry and shrink on to the rims, further strengthening the wheel. Each 90-cm-diameter wheel was fastened to an axle of ash wood or tamarind with a small lynch pin. Unlike the chariots of their enemies, the Egyptians moved the axle to the very back of the cab in an effort to balance the vehicle and improve its manoeuvrability. The axle was much longer than the 1 metre width of the cab and this wide, 1.75-metre wheel base will have provided enhanced stability and handling on the tight turns upon which the Egyptian chariot tactics were based.

A chariot without horses is just expensively curved timber, and so a draught pole, steam-bent and typically of elm wood, linked the chariot cab with the motive power of the two-horse team. This 2.5-metre-length pole ran beneath the floor of the cab and was fastened there by rawhide straps. It then curved upwards to meet a yoke of willow wood to which the two horses would be secured. Horses were yoked to the pole and the yoke rested on a leather saddle fastened high up at the base of the animal's neck. Reins used by the chariot driver to control the team fed through loops on the saddle, then passed up to a bridle. Pharaohs are often depicted alone in the chariot, with the reins of both horses tied around their waist, a simple artistic technique that did not clutter the scene with an unimportant chariot driver. Ramses II actually records a conversation he had with his own driver, Menna, in the epic poem celebrating the victory at Kadesh, proof that the tying of reins around the waist was something of an artistic convention. Some chariot horses wear what appear to be blinkers, limiting their field of view in an attempt to reduce panic in the war horse. Two horse skeletons have been found, both dating from the Eighteenth Dynasty, and the earlier animal, found at Soleb, belongs to an animal of comparatively small size (13.2 hands). The second skeleton had been buried at Deir el-Bahri near the tomb of Senemut and this example measured 14 hands (around 130 cm). Like chariots and composite bows, healthy war horses were a valuable tribute demanded by Egypt of those Asiatic states that it had conquered. Tuthmosis III received 924 chariot horses from the kingdom of Mitanni after his victory at the Battle of Megiddo in 1,456 BC.

Armour seems to have been worn by horses in Ramses II's army at Kadesh, and the horses of Tutankhamun that appear on his inlaid box are likewise fully protected. A textile trapper was overlain with a coat of bronze scales that alternate with lines of brightly painted scales, creating an attractively striped pattern. Trappers were tied underneath the horses belly by fabric ties. The necks of horses also appear to be protected by rows of leather bands, perhaps also fitted with bronze scales. Not all chariot horses were armoured and it is clear that light chariot forces, used for scouting and reconnaissance, had no need of this expensive protection.

Quivers were attached to the outer body of a chariot cab, and the Florence chariot was fitted with a single forward-facing quiver on each side. By the reign of Seti I, an additional pair of quivers had been added to the cab, each holding a pair of javelins. Ceremonial chariots were discovered within the tomb of Tutankhamun that were gilded with gold leaf and inlaid with precious stones. This type of ornamental chariot is sometimes referred to in Egyptian texts and it was not just gold, but also silver and even electrum (an alloy of silver and gold) that were used to decorate the royal vehicles.

Chariots were complex structures, employing a number of woods not native to Egypt, as well as advanced techniques for bending and shaping the timbers. Special chariot workshops were established for their manufacture—the Eighteenth Dynasty tomb of Hapu illustrates one such workshop, with some men fashioning the rims and others the spokes, while another group of craftsmen assemble the wheels. Even the leather parts, such as the quivers and bow cases, were made here and then attached to the assembled vehicle. When in the field, it was important that craftsmen were on hand to maintain and repair the army's chariots. Wheels and axles were prone to breakages and so repair workshops were established at waystations on well-travelled military routes. A letter received by the military governor of Ta'anach in the fifteenth century BC relayed a request for repair parts: 'I was ambushed in Gurra; so give me this day two chariot wheels and an axle or two.... And when the making of the axle has been completed, send it to me...'

On campaign, far from outposts and city garrisons, mobile workshops were used to maintain the pharaoh's chariot corps. A relief showing Ramses II's camp at Kadesh includes a small vignette—an artificer is assisted by two of his apprentices as he repairs a chariot pole. This same relief also illustrates some of the more mundane transport vehicles employed by the army whilst on campaign. Oxen are hitched to heavy two-wheeled carts, and the bodies of these carts are square in shape and feature rounded covers across the top.

Siege Operations

Then, as now, the Fertile Crescent proved to be a crossroads where the people of Egypt, Anatolia, Mesopotamia, Arabia, and the mountains of Armenia could meet, trade, and fight. To remain in this region, unmolested by the great powers who were constantly vying for control, a community had to defend itself with walls, battlements, towers, and gateways—the fortified city dominated urban life in the Bronze Age Near East for many centuries. It was the long duration of habitation at these sites that was responsible for the 'tell' or mound-city, which, by the Late Bronze Age, sat on dozens of past phases of the same settlement. Raised up in this way after centuries of rebuilding and reconstruction, most of the cities on Syria and Palestine sat upon their own defensive hills. Typically, a city, like Hazor, was made up of a large lower city that was defended by a substantial wall constructed of brick and pierced by a small number of heavily fortified gateways. Within the city, at its highest point, sat a heavily defended upper city or acropolis within which the king and his officials, the royal guards, and the most wealthy and influential members of the community lived.

The sides of the tell or hill were not left as unconsolidated rubble, but hard-packed and reinforced to provide a steep and inaccessible slope designed to deter the siege operations of any would-be attacker. Some cities (such as Tell el-'Ajjul and Hazor) added a wide and deep ditch to their outermost defences. The ditch at Tell el-'Ajjul was of impressive dimensions—10 metres in depth and 15 metres wide. The gradient of the outer slope (*glacis*) was often so steep and the gateway through the city walls so high above the surrounding countryside (Hazor's gateway, for example, sat 25 metres above the plain) that a long path climbed obliquely around the embankment beneath the city walls to reach the gate. Any attacker wanting to enter the city by this route had to withstand a tremendous barrage of missile fire from the attackers ranged along these walls. Each gateway led directly into the lower city through several defensive chambers and sets of doors.

Remarkably, although the Egyptians successfully besieged many Canaanite cities, there is not a single reference to a battering ram, the key weapon that came to dominate siege warfare for the next 2,000 years. Instead, Egyptian soldiers are shown climbing scaling ladders in their attempt to gain access to the city under siege. A battle relief from the temple of Amun at Karnak depicts troops from Ramses II's army besieging Ashkelon in southern Palestine. While a phalanx of infantrymen rout a force of Canaanite defenders in front of the walls, other troops scale ladders with their shields slung across their backs or storm the wooden gates with their battle axes. The besieged appear terrified, praying to their gods and lifting trapped individuals up to the safety of the balconies and battlements of the acropolis. A similar story is told by a relief from the Ramesseum in Thebes; here, the Syrian city of Deper is being held by the Hittites, and Egyptian forces are massed at the walls. While a violent chariot battle is being waged nearby on the plain, Egyptian hand-to-hand soldiers (including several royal princes) begin their assault. Archers provide covering fire while men climb scaling ladders to reach the battlements. Hittite defenders use spears to oppose the attack and some of their archers try to pick off individual Egyptian warriors. One figure is shown about to throw a heavy stone over the battlement onto the massed Egyptian troops. In the chaos, several Hittites tumble from the parapets, victims of Egyptian archery, while in a scene reminiscent of the Ashkelon siege relief, defenders desperate to escape the attacking troops are being pulled up to the safety of towers and battlements on ropes. This tactic was famously used by the king of Kadesh and the ruler of Megiddo to escape from Tuthmosis III at the Battle of Megiddo in 1,456 BC. The Annals of Tuthmosis III describe this event: 'They abandoned their horses and their chariots of gold and silver, so that someone might draw them up into this town by hoisting on their garments. Now the people had shut this town against them, but they let down their garments to hoist them up into this town'.

Direct and concerted efforts to scale the walls of an enemy city or to hack down its gates would not always work, and in some situations, a city was besieged for months or even years. Pharaoh Ahmose, in his attempt to take the Hyksos city off Sharuhen in their Palestinian homeland, laid siege to the city for three consecutive years. Megiddo might have fallen to the troops of Tuthmosis III quickly had they not been distracted by plunder on the battlefield. The siege of the city that followed lasted for seven months.

Long-term sieges may have resulted in fewer immediate casualties among the attacking force; however, they involved a large logistical operation to support several armed camps around the enemy city and a vigilant defence to guard against hostile sallies from within the walls. The Annals of Tuthmosis III describe the establishment of a siege camp around Megiddo following the failure to capture it during the battle. First, its dimensions were measured out and a defensive ditch was dug around it. A thick timber palisade was then constructed from fruit trees in the surrounding area. Finally, sentries were posted who would not permit the passage of the enemy, except for deserters, who could be let through to the Egyptian lines. This grand fortification was given a name, '*Menkheperre-is-the-Surrounder-of-the-Asiatics*'—just as medieval men-at-arms christened the trebuchet's and cannon of their own day.

The building of siege works from trees on the plain is also described in the Biblical book Deuteronomy:

> In case you lay siege to a city many days by fighting against it so as to capture it, you must not ruin its (fruit) trees by wielding an axe against them.... Only a tree that you know is not a tree for food is the one you should ruin and you must cut it down and build siege works against the city that is making war with you—until it falls.
>
> Deuteronomy 20:19-20

The Navy

There were two types of naval vessel in use during the New Kingdom, the naval transport and the warship. There is little evidence for warships before the Nineteenth Dynasty, although amphibious operations are certainly recorded. During Ahmose's campaign against the Hyksos in the Egyptian Delta, ships were used to transport

The siege of a Canaanite city by a Nineteenth Dynasty Egyptian army. A phalanx of infantrymen engage local soldiers in front of the city, while other troops climb siege ladders or cut through the wooden gate.

troops to the battlefield via the twisting watercourses of that region. Tuthmosis III, as part of the preparations for his campaign into Syria, constructed a large fleet of ships at Perunefer, near Memphis. Cargo vessels were loaded up here with supplies, arms, and men for the journey along the Palestinian and Syrian coast in support of the armies that were marching northwards along the Way of the Sea. Tuthmosis was the first pharaoh to utilise his naval forces in this way, to project Egyptian power across the Near East rapidly in support of other forces.

As we have seen, the navy had been an integral part of Egyptian military operations for centuries and a posting to this service brought with it great status. The establishment of a chariot corps at the start of the Eighteenth Dynasty, and the rise of a new class of land-holding chariot-nobles to man it, effectively stole the glamour of the navy. Yet it proved still to be formidable arm of the Egyptian state, as Tuthmosis III's innovative use of amphibious tactics proved.

During the Nineteenth Dynasty, the warship (as opposed to the military transport ship) proved itself in Egyptian service against the Sea Peoples. In 1,187 BC, a large flotilla of Sea Peoples' ships arrived at the Delta and it was met by an Egyptian squadron intent on destroying it. The hostile naval force was most likely made up of mercenaries and northern tribes, although the flotilla may actually have been a convoy of settlers and refugees, in just the way the land element of the 1,187 BC attack had been, with its wagons, families, and children.

Reliefs at Ramses III's temple at Medinet Habu, on the west bank of Thebes, illustrate in some detail this unique naval battle. Ships on either side clash at close quarters and soldiers are able to target one another directly. Depictions of the naval engagement on the walls at Medinet Habu are remarkable, nothing like them survives from the New Kingdom. Warships manned by the Sea Peoples crash into the Egyptian vessels, which fight back with slingers positioned in the ships' crow's nests. The fighting rages at the mouth of the Delta, so close to shore that Egyptian archers on the river banks are able to shoot at the enemy on board their boats. The pharaoh declared:

> ...I caused the river mouth to be prepared like a strong wall with warships, transports and merchantmen, they were manned entirely from bow to stern with brave fighting men and their weapons.

Ramses III recorded that ships of all types were used in the defence if the Delta, but only warships were depicted. These Egyptian warships are shown with both oars and sails, while the vessels of the *Shekelesh*, *Denyen*, and *Weshwesh* are depicted only with sails. The enemy vessels are not depicted with oars, although they must have had them because the square sail with which they are equipped lacked the ability to tack. Were the oars shipped in combat? If the rowers doubled as oarsmen, as was the practice among the Bronze Age Greeks, then the artist may be representing this fact. If the enemy vessels did lack oars,

Detail from a relief at Medinet Habu depicting an Egyptian warship at the battle of the Nile Delta.

then the advantage of manoeuvrability lay with the Egyptians, who could move more freely to attack or avoid the attacks of their foes through the work of the soldiers assigned as rowers. Indeed, the crew of one Egyptian ship, at the lower right of the relief, is actually back-sculling after snagging a ship full of Sea Peoples—the ship is shown capsizing, with its arrow-shot crew tangled up in the sail and rigging. No Egyptian ship is shown ramming an enemy vessel, but the lion-head prow looks very much like an ancient ram that Bronze Age Greek ships of this date certainly possessed. As a point of interest, Egyptologist Anthony Spallinger has noted that the high sides of the Egyptian galleys, behind which the rowers' shelter, is not known in Nile naval technology; rather, it is more of an Aegean Bronze Age tradition. Clearly, the military planners of the late Nineteenth Dynasty were looking northwards for inspiration for their ship designs, or were perhaps even hiring Greek shipbuilders to fit out their fleet.

Both navies pack the decks of their ships with fighting men. Egyptian warships, as depicted at Medinet Habu, were streamlined and crescent-shaped and propelled by a bank of oars. Numbers vary from ship to ship on the relief, but there will have been around twenty oars per ship; a similar vessel used on a trading mission to Ethiopia in the reign of Queen Hatshepsut had thirty oars with thirty rowers, as well as a crew of eight sailors. Steering was effected via a pair of large rudder boards that were controlled from a raised aft deck. At the prow, a raised foredeck allowed marines to gather, either to attack an opposing vessel with archery or to make ready to storm across should the ships collide. The Egyptian vessels each had a central mast, although the sail was raised during combat to minimise damage and allow the archers a fuller field of fire. A crow's nest is shown at the top of each mast and the look-out within is armed with a sling in each case.

APPENDIX I

Building the Shields

Over the past decade, I have reconstructed a large amount of ancient military material in an effort to study its use, design, and method of construction. Much of my work has involved the fabrication of Roman military equipment, from belts and arrows to clothing, shields, tents, satchels, and greaves. It was a desire of mine to reconstruct some part of the Egyptian soldier's military kit and, in particular, the shields of the New Kingdom. The evidence from reliefs and from the shields discovered within the tomb of Tutankhamun indicate a change in the shape of shields between the Eighteenth and Nineteenth Dynasties.

I planned to construct both Egyptian shields using authentic materials, and, rather than employ my most efficient modern electrical tools, I decided to also use authentic Egyptian carpentry tools. As luck would have it, I had created a Bronze Age carpenter's tool kit several years earlier for a school exhibit. All of my tools were based on examples held within the British Museum and were made of thick brass sheet or brass wire mounted on wooden tool handles. Bronze and brass are similar substances; bronze is an alloy of copper mixed with a little tin (10 per cent is typical), while brass alloys copper with zinc. Archaeologists often refer to bronze objects as 'copper alloy' because of the many other elements that can be mixed up with brass or bronze, ranging from arsenic, phosphorus, zinc, silicon, and manganese. Egyptian copper was mined in Sinai and this metal contained amounts of arsenic, producing a mixed bronze alloy.

The carpentry tools that I had ready at my disposal included a handsaw, a bow drill, an awl, a smoothing stone, and a chisel. The saw was simply made from a sheet of brass, with its teeth cut crudely into the cutting edge. This was a 'pull saw' that did not have the cutting power or efficiency of a modern wood saw, which has teeth that project sideways away from the main blade and that work both on the 'push' stroke and 'pull' stroke. Cutting wood with the Egyptian saw required a lot more effort than with a modern example.

The bow drill is a two-part tool—the drill is a screwdriver-like object with a wooden handle and a brass point that will be twisted rapidly back and forth to drill down slowly into the wood. This was not done by hand; instead, a leather thong was wrapped around the handle and attached to a small wooden bow. By sawing this bow backwards and forwards, the leather thong rotates the drill at high speed. It is commonly associated with prehistoric societies as a method of starting fires (the brass drill bit replaced, in those cases, with a hardwood point).

Awls are simply bronze or brass spikes mounted on short handles that are used to make holes in wood or leather. My awl was used primarily in punching holes through each shield's rawhide edging.

Smoothing stones were used *in lieu* of rasps and files, and although sandpaper did not exist in ancient times, I have been able to reproduce its effects by dipping cloth first into olive oil and then into sand, which adheres to the fabric. My smoothing stone is a coarse beach stone picked up locally. The final tool in my Egyptian carpenter's kit is a chisel, which requires either the use of a wooden mallet or a hammer stone.

Both shields were constructed from three planks of beech wood, 7 mm in thickness. Once cut to shape, I boiled up finely cut pieces of rawhide to make a gooey, brown glue. I used this, along with wooden pegs driven into drilled holes, to join the three planks together. Each shield needed a handgrip, which I cut and shaped from two more pieces of wood, pegging and gluing them in place. Informative reliefs from the tombs of Hapu and Rekhmire illustrate activity within a shield-making workshop. They clearly show Eighteenth Dynasty shields being made, and being covered with leather hide that was first stretched over a frame. I used two goatskins to cover the faces of the shields, using more of the hide glue to stick them firmly in place. Once dry, authentic designs could be painted on to the faces.

A detailed and colourful rendition of a shield appears in the tomb of Kenamon, from the reign of Amenhotep II, and I used this as a model for my Eighteenth Dynasty shield. It is patterned after an actual cow hide, harking back to Old Kingdom and Middle Kingdom military traditions, although these later shield patterns were only painted to simulate the mottling of cow hide, often in bright and highly unrealistic colours. The Kenamon shield is decorated with a blue 'cowhide' design. Paints used were modern, but chalk-based, giving a thick earthy texture to the painting.

My longer and more straight-sided Ramesside shield features a brass sun disc nailed to the centre of the upper face. I used brass dome-headed tacks for this task, which provide an additional decorative effect. Rather than paint the Ramesside shield in bold colours, I left it white and edged it with red and blue, in imitation of Nineteenth and Twentieth Dynasty shields depicted on tomb paintings. My intention had been to produce two brass cobras that would decorate the flanks of the disc; however, limited by the Bronze Age technology at my disposal and my own limited metalworking skills, I had to instead resort to painting these on. Cutting shapes out of brass sheet is done without the benefit of modern angle-grinders or stainless steel tin snips. Instead, I used the traditional method of chiselling to cut out my sun disc, hammering the chisel down vertically to cut through the brass sheet.

Hundreds of individual strikes were needed to cut out the disc. I could not achieve enough accuracy with the chisel to cut out the sinuous form of the snake.

Before I turned to edging the two shields, I addressed the problem of attaching a shoulder strap to the Nineteenth Dynasty shield, just like those shown on siege reliefs, where individual Egyptian soldiers have slung their shields on to their backs. My experience with Roman shield construction taught me that simply tying a length of leather cord to the grip does not work very well—the shield tips sideways—and none of the Egyptian reliefs show slung shields adopting that attitude. To maintain the shield's upright posture, I decided to mount a metal loop on the inside of the shield board at the ten o'clock position. I used the bow drill to bore a hole through the plank and began to hammer on the loop using a brass rivet, but I was not satisfied; the loop worked, yet it smacked of over-engineering and may have been something that the Roman army did—but not typically something that the metal-poor Egyptians would have done. Bronze was just too valuable to be put to such a frivolous use. So I removed the brass loop and decided instead to use a simple loop of leather cord, knotted through the hole in the shield-board. Now it looked more like an individual soldier's *ad hoc* improvisation—and I was much happier with the results. An Egyptian infantryman need only take his leather shoulder strap and tie one end onto the hand grip and the other onto the leather loop projecting out of the back of his shield. By untying the two ends, he could just as easily remove the shoulder strap.

Edging the shield is always necessary. A single strike from the axe or sword of an opponent could split open a plank and splinter the shield. During the height of the Roman army, the legions edged their shields with bronze strips; later, this gave way to reinforcements of rawhide, stitched around the shield edge and left to harden and dry. Rawhide is an extremely tough and durable material when dry, the perfect way to strengthen the vulnerable edge of a combat shield. There are models of Old Kingdom shields in both the Louvre, Paris, and the New York Metropolitan Museum of Art, and these scale models are all edged with a strip of rawhide stitched on with thread. I was able to get hold of large sheets of bovine rawhide (animal skin that has been cleaned and stretched, but not tanned). The rawhide was soaked in order to soften it enough to be cut into strips. Holes were bored around the shield edge with the bow drill and the rawhide strips put in place. I used the awl to puncture holes in the rawhide that lined up with the pre-drilled holes and then began stitching it in place using waxed linen thread.

After twelve hours, the rawhide had dried, tightened, and hardened and was ready for a coat of paint, enabling it to blend seamlessly into the shield's applied decoration. The shields were finished and, due to the relatively scarce amount of metal involved in their construction, they were pretty light (at least compared to the large Roman shields that I was more used to building and carrying). The blue Eighteenth Dynasty shield weighed 1.9 kg, while the white Ramesside shield weighed 3 kg due to its larger size and decorative metal disc.

APPENDIX II

Military Glossary

aamu	throwstick; also people of Asia ('throwstick-folk')
ahautyu	full time soldiers
bagsu	dagger
dja	spear
ger'iu	shield-bearer/ charioteer
gurpisu sparri	helmet (Akkadian term)
hedj	mace
hery Medjay	Chief of Medjay
hewenu-nefru	young recruits
hikau khasut	Princes of the Desert Uplands (the 'Hyksos')
hupshu	peasant conscripts (Canaanite term)
humty	'women warriors' derogatory term for Hittites
idnu	military deputy, or adjutant
ikem	shield
ikhu	axe
kedjen	shield-bearer/ charioteer
kedjen-tepy	First Charioteer
kenyt-nesu	King's Braves, an elite unit
khopesh	bronze scimitar
mahut	spear-shaft
maryannu	Canaanite chariot warriors
mesha	army division
menfyt	seasoned veteran soldier
nakhtu-aa	'strong-arm fighters', hand-to-hand soldiers
ne'arin	elite type of troops (Canaanite term)
nefru	recruit
neken	sword
nemes	royal striped head-cloth
nesyut	javelin
neyut	militia
nomarch	provincial governor
pah' ahat	Egyptian naval fleet
pedjet	archery bow; also army 'host'
peherer	chariot runner
pekheret	frontier patrol
peri	battlefield
qenyeh	white banded textile armour
rww	'sea lands'
sa	army company
sekheperu	drill company
seneny	chariot warrior
seser	arrow
tiryana	coat of bronze scale armour
tjai-seryt	standard bearer
uraeus	royal cobra headdress
wehenu	herald

Bibliography

Aldred, C., *The Egyptians*, (Thames and Hudson, 1961)

Astour, M., 'Ḫattusilisˇ, Ḫalab, and Ḫanigalbat', *Journal of Near Eastern Studies*, 31.2, pp. 102-109 (1972)

Baines, J., and Malek, J., *Atlas of Ancient Egypt*, (Andromeda Oxford, 1996)

Binst, O. (ed.), *The Levant*, (Ko:neman, 1999)

Blackman, A. M., and Peet, T. E., 'Papyrus Lansing: A Translation with Notes', *The Journal of Egyptian Archaeology*, 11, pp. 284-298 (1925)

Booth, C., *The Hyksos Period in Egypt*, (Shire, 2005)

Breasted, J. H., *Ancient Records of Egypt Vol. 2 and 3*, (University of Chicago Press, 1906)

Clayton, P., *Chronicle of the Pharaohs*, (Thames and Hudson, 1994)

Davies, W. V., *Catalogue of Egyptian Antiquities in the British Museum, VII: Tools and Weapons 1: Axes*, (British Museum, 1987)

Donadoni, S., *The Egyptians*, (University of Chicago, 1990)

Drews, R., *The End of the Bronze Age*, (Princeton University Press, 1993)

Faulkner, R. O., 'The Battle of Megiddo', *The Journal of Egyptian Archaeology*, 28, pp. 2-15. (1942)

Faulkner, R. O., 'Egyptian Military Organisation', *The Journal of Egyptian Archaeology*, 39, pp. 32-47. (1953)

Fields, N., *Soldier of the Pharaoh*, (Osprey, 2007)

Gabriel, R. A., and Metz, K. S., *From Sumer to Rome: The Military Capabilities of Ancient Armies* (Praeger, 1991)

Gardiner, A. H., *The Kadesh Inscriptions of Ramesses II*, (Griffith Institute, 1960)

Goedicke, H., *The Battle of Megiddo*, (Halgo, 2000)

Gurney, O. R., *The Hittites*, (Penguin, 1954)

Hall, R., *Egyptian Textiles*, (Shire, 1986)

Harris, J. E., and Weeks, K., *X-Raying the Pharaohs*, (Charles Scribner's Sons., 1973)

Healy, M., *New Kingdom Egypt*, (Osprey, 1992)

Janssen, J., and R. M., *Growing Up in Ancient Egypt*, (Rubicon, 1990)

Keegan, J., *The Face of Battle*, (Jonathan Cape, 1976)

Lichtheim, M., *Ancient Egyptian Literature,* (University of California Press, 1976)

Littauer, M. A., and Crouwel, J. H., *Chariots and Related Equipment from the Tomb of Tut'ankhamun*, (Griffith Institute, 1985)

Macqueen, J. G., *The Hittites*, (Thames and Hudson, 1986)

McDermott, B., *Warfare in Ancient Egypt*, (Sutton, 2004)

McLeod, W. E., *Composite Bows from the Tomb of Tut'ankhamun*, (Griffith Institute, 1970)

Murnane, W. J., *The Road to Kadesh: A Historical Interpretation of the Battle Reliefs of King Sety I at Karnak*, (Chicago Oriental Institute, 1985)

Partridge, R. B., *Fighting Pharaohs: Weapons and Warfare in Ancient Egypt*, (Peartree, 2002)

Pritchard, J. (Ed.), Atlas of the Bible, (HarperCollins, 1987)

Reeves, C., *Egyptian Medicine*, (Shire, 1992)

Shaw, G. J., 'The Death of King Seqenenre Tao', *Journal of the American Research Center in Egypt*, 45. (2009)

Shaw, I., *Egyptian Warfare and Weapons*, (Shire, 1991)

Spalinger, A. J., *War in Ancient Egypt*, (Blackwell, 2005)

Spruytte, J., *Early Harness Systems: Experimental Studies*, (J.A. Allen, 1983)

Stead, M., *Egyptian Life*, (British Museum, 1986)

Stillman, N., and Tallis, N., *Armies of the Ancient Near East: 3000 to 539 BC*, (WRG, 1984)

Taylor, J. H., *Egypt and Nubia*, (British Museum, 1991)

Shaw, I., and Nicholson, P., *British Museum Dictionary of Ancient Egypt*, (BCA, 1995)

Vogel, C., 'Fallen Heroes? Winlock's 'slain soldiers' reconsidered', *The Journal of Egyptian Archaeology*, 89, pp. 239-245, (2003)

Wilkinson, J. G., *The Ancient Egyptians, Their Life and Customs*, (John Murray, 1853)

Wilkinson, R. H., *Symbol and Magic in Egyptian Art*, (Thames and Hudson, 1994)

Wilson, H., *Egyptian Food and Drink*, (Shire, 2001)

Winlock, H. E., *The Slain Soldiers of Ned-Hepet-Re' Mentu-Hotep*, (Metropolitan Museum of Art, 1945)

Yadin, Y., *The Art of Warfare in Biblical Lands*, (Weidenfeld and Nicolson, 1963)

Index